# La Cuisine Chantraine

# La Cuisine Chantraine

*The Complete Collection
of Original Recipes Created at
the Restaurant Chantraine
in Brussels* 〜

By Charles Chantraine 〜

*M. Barrows & Company, Inc.*
*New York*      *1966*
*distributed by William Morrow & Company, Inc.*

# To my dear wife, Yvonne

She inspired me to persevere
and was my courageous collaborator
in the long task of creating this book.
Without her constant and affectionate presence,
it would never have been written.

# Preface

THE CUISINE of a country is like art and good manners. It reveals more about that country than all long historical and economic treatises put together. It gives a valuable and usually quite accurate picture of the feelings and even of fundamental principles that the people of a nation share.

Thus one can say that Maître Chantraine has been able to show with his art something of what the Belgian spirit is like. Those—and they are many—who have been privileged to taste his cooking in the tiny confines of his restaurant know exactly what we mean.

Monsieur Chantraine has not reiterated the local and national dishes in his kitchen. Far from that. Inheritor to the great tradition of master-chefs, to whom so much gratitude is owed by us all, he has elevated the standard of his daily work to that of art, with results that are superb and universal in their aspirations. For, say what you will, it is clear that there is an affinity between what goes on in that charming little establishment on the Rue des Harengs, just a step away from one of the most beautiful city squares in the world, and a nation whose love of life and pride in good and beautiful things have given to our civilization a treasury of works of art of every kind.

We have often expressed to Maître Chantraine our own gratitude to him, on behalf, as well, of all those who love this their native land and wish others to do the same. On the propitious occasion of the publication of his book, we express our gratitude to him once more, knowing that his words will carry far beyond the borders of his own country the reputation earned by all our master craftsmen and artists.

ARTHUR HAULOT
Commissaire Général
au Tourisme de Belgique

# Mise en Scène

IN A NARROW street in Brussels called the Rue des Harengs
(Herring Street) just off the historical and beautiful Grand'
Place, nestled inconspicuously among other houses much like it,
stands a little restaurant known to travelers from the world
around. It is the oldest restaurant in Belgium, having been built
in 1660 on the site of an establishment of even earlier fame,
the Cabaret de Charles-Quint. The present structure, which still
contains the original seventeenth-century oaken beams, is a
*monument historique* preserved by the City of Brussels.

Throughout the centuries, the restaurant has changed character
many times. It started as a humble hostelry, under the name of
L'Esturgeon, specializing in fish, oysters and beer. By the middle
of the nineteenth century, it had been transformed into a first-
class restaurant and had taken the title of L'Épaule de Mouton—
a legend the building still bears in red letters on its narrow four-
story façade.

Its present fame, however, is due entirely to the activities of
the Chantraine family which took over the restaurant shortly
after the turn of the century. It is known in Brussels today as
the Restaurant Chantraine, where this one family has been in
charge for almost fifty years.

The father of the present proprietor, Charles Chantraine,
Père, started his activities in 1907, with a brother-in-law, Monsieur René, and the tradition is now being carried on by the son,
Charles, and his wife, and the same Oncle René. In a small high-
ceilinged dining room, hung with mementoes of past genera-
tions and more recent testimonials from appreciative patrons,
the Chantraines continue to produce incomparable food, much

of it prepared in full view of the diners. In the center of the room there is a small stove, and on it, in shining copper pans of all sizes and shapes and with a few favorite utensils, Oncle René does the final cooking for every dish that is served. With savory preparations that come to him from the kitchen, and with rich cream, fresh butter, good mustard, salt, a busy pepper mill, and wines and liqueurs of every description, he performs miracles with a deftness and a cheerful calm that are a wonder to behold. With great good will he gladly answers any questions, hiding none of his knowledge. But it is obvious that the early, behind-the-scene preparations are as important as these later, visible rites. It is the secrets of both that the master-chef, Charles Chantraine, imparts in the following pages.

The main body of his book is devoted to original recipes created by the Chantraines, father, uncle, and son. They have worked, these fifty years, in the classic tradition. The foundations of their skill will be familiar to anyone who has taken an interest in great European cuisine. But, and this is no less in the classic tradition, they have been originators and creators, using the established disciplines to produce dishes entirely their own. They list the impressive total of *"90 Créations Culinaires Exclusives"* on their menu, most of them available every day, either on the daily menu or to your order, a few of them limited by the seasons of the year.

One would go to the Restaurant Chantraine for an important occasion. So, also, should one cook from this book for special occasions. And yet, no fine cuisine is altogether elaborate. Simplicity and the most practical of kitchen techniques are always part of it as well. Therefore, the attentive reader will find in Maître Chantraine's book many simple dishes that are carefully considered, rather than intricate, and intricate recipes that are made feasible by the practical knowledge of cooks of long experience. Though it represents decades of work and training, it is a short and approachable volume from which you can choose, whatever your skill as a cook, a select repertory of dishes not to be found anywhere else which will become the specialties of your own house. And, it is the author's hope, your success with his more modest preparations will tempt you to proceed to more challenging recipes that he and his family have so long labored to perfect.

# Contents

# Introduction

COOKING, most particularly the creation of original dishes, is a demanding art. Just as in music, painting, or architecture, the artist must have special knowledge and a particular sensitivity. To build a culinary art of one's own requires experience, patience, and care.

As is true of every art, cooking varies from place to place, through the years fashions change and cooking, too, must change and even at times be revolutionized. But since it appeals to the senses as well as to the mind, and since palate and stomach are not easily fooled, cooking must be fundamentally honest. It must be free from complicated artifice and unnecessary extremes or it will quickly be exposed as inferior.

Nor, however, must it be limited only to what is considered classic in culinary art. To lean always on the famous regional dishes or the established recipes of tradition is to standardize ones art. My experience has been that the right way to cook is to draw ones inspiration from many sources, both old and new, and from many regions and countries. The directing principle is to adopt all that is of value and never to exclude anything of quality. This and the disdain of false elaboration are the rules that have governed the Chantraine cuisine.

I long considered that it was my province to perform my art to the best of my ability and that I should leave the writing of cookbooks to others. However, many friends of long standing, my dear wife, and so many of the guests at our restaurant, from all parts of the world, who have honored us with their compliments—all these kind people finally persuaded me to write these recipes for publication. Their argument has been that our cooking should be enjoyed by others in their own homes as well as in our restaurant and that many who may not have the good fortune to visit Belgium would never know of the work we have done here unless LA CUISINE CHANTRAINE were published.

And so, the writing of this book was undertaken. The result of this labor is a small volume that is in no sense a comprehensive cookbook but is instead the collection of our family's original recipes, created by my father, my uncle, and myself. It includes a section on basic preparations that are common to all fine cooking.

LA CUISINE CHANTRAINE is dedicated to my wife in particular, to my family and friends in general, and to all those who encouraged me to write it. We hope it will bring pleasure to those who read it and that in time we may hear echoes of satisfaction from those who use it.

Since this is my art, I have followed an old custom that will perhaps not be unfamiliar to you and dedicated many of the recipes to those who have befriended me, my family, and, on occasion, my country.

CHARLES CHANTRAINE

# La Cuisine Chantraine

# I

## Fonds de Cuisine
*Basic Preparations & Ingredients*

## Menus
*The Sequence of Courses in a Menu*

THE RECIPES for basic preparations and *fonds de cuisine* that are so important in our cooking are given in Chapter VIII, arranged in appropriate categories depending on whether their primary use is for meat, fish, garnishing, or sweets. There are not a great many of them, but they have been placed together for convenient reference, as they are repeatedly called for as ingredients in our recipes. The connoisseur will recognize that most of these basic preparations are classic elements of cooking; a few have been especially created by us.

The *fonds de cuisine* present certain problems for inexperienced cooks or in an average household where the time and equipment for making them may simply not be available. Not all these basic preparations are difficult, but such things as the authentic CLEAR MEAT CONSOMMÉ, MEAT JELLY, CONCENTRATED FISH STOCK, or LOBSTER BISQUE BASE are demanding to make. They are made as a matter of course in a restaurant kitchen, but we sincerely wish this book to be useful to busy housekeepers as well as interesting to connoisseurs, so we have carefully considered the matter of substitutions and proposed their use frequently in writing our recipes.

This is by no means to suggest that the same results can be achieved by using commercially prepared substitutes for authentic *fonds de cuisine*. It stands to reason that these preparations, made with care and skill in one's own kitchen, cannot be approached in flavor and quality by commercial products. You need only to look briefly at the instructions for making them to see that this must be so.

One of the most interesting purposes of basic preparations should be explained. Remember that, in a restaurant kitchen, we solve problems far more complex than anything that normally needs to be done in a home kitchen. Therefore many of the methods we have developed are of the utmost practicality. Consider that, every day, we serve many people a wide variety of dishes at different hours of the day and evening. *Fonds de cuisine* and other ingredients prepared in advance are as useful in solving these problems as they are important in maintaining high standards of cooking.

You will see in our recipes that the time-consuming work is very often done in advance. With your ingredients and basic preparations ready, to assemble the finished dish requires care but is not a complicated matter. You will see that this is a general method that applies to both simple and complex dishes. It has nothing to do with "short-cuts" that sacrifice quality. On the contrary, its purpose is to produce a perfect dish, which in a restaurant cannot be done at all unless it is done efficiently.

I believe that this approach to cooking can be most useful to home cooks. Setting aside, temporarily, the difficulty of making yourself some of the basic preparations, consider exploring this method, using the best possible commercial substitutes for the *fonds de cuisine* or other preparations called for. It will be an illuminating experience for you to draw on this reserve of prepared ingredients to assemble a dish which you might otherwise have considered beyond your powers as either a too busy or possibly too inexperienced cook. To demonstrate this point, I would encourage you at first to use some commercial or other substitutes. Though I am quite certain the dish will not be the ideal one we wish you to taste, it will be very good and will tempt you then to try it again with the authentic basic preparations.

We come now to making these preparations yourself. Note, first, that they keep well under refrigeration and that, second, they are used again and again in many and quite different dishes. Therefore, the labor of making adequate quantities of one or several *fonds de cuisine* will provide you with ingredients to make a series of our specialties at their best instead of second best. There is no doubt that, for anyone who must entertain frequently or who must cook often for whatever reason, this supply of basic preparations is a great convenience.

Furthermore, you need not necessarily make the large quantities in the recipes for some of the *fonds de cuisine.* They may be reduced as long as the proportions of the ingredients are maintained. We have given our full recipes because we know from experience that they produce precisely the results we want. To reduce them can introduce a certain element of uncertainty. But the quantities for some are evidently larger than are practical for a household where a great deal of cooking is not being done, and you should prepare quantities that are sensible for your purposes.

Finally, if somewhat reluctantly, I indicate the substitutions that we have agreed upon for the authentic *fonds de cuisine:*

For CLEAR MEAT CONSOMMÉ, p. 141, you may use our alternative recipes for QUICK MEAT CONSOMMÉ, p. 144, or CHICKEN CONSOMMÉ, p. 145, Or, commercial products sold in tins. This is a last resort, but such products of fine quality do exist and your aim must simply be to buy the best. Be careful of overseasoned or oversweet commercial consommés.

For MEAT JELLY, p. 145, or *glace de viande,* no true substitute exists, but commercial meat extracts or meat glazes, again of the best quality you know of, can be used. They will be salted, as meat jelly is not, and therefore must be used sparingly, in lesser quantities than indicated for meat jelly in our recipes. *Glace de viande* of authentic quality is available in a few very fine food stores, sometimes only on order. It may also tend to be somewhat salty, but if you can find it you are fortunate, as this is not only one of our most important ingredients, it is also, we must confess, one of the most time-consuming to make. Do not be disturbed at its fairly high cost, as it is used in very small quantities and lasts a long time.

For PÂTÉ PLUS-QUE-PARFAIT, p. 15, which is a pâté we serve by itself as well as require in several recipes, commercial liver pâtés can be substituted. A tinned *foie gras* or *pâté de foie gras* would be excellent, of course, though much more expensive than making our pâté. We must leave it to you to decide what other liver pâté or fine liverwurst is the best grade available to you. Again, you must beware of excessive saltiness.

COURT-BOUILLON FOR FISH, p. 149, needs no substitute; it is a simple preparation. CONCENTRATED FISH STOCK or *fumet de poisson,* p. 150, is derived from it and, if you do not make the concentrated stock, a small quantity of *court-bouillon* may be reduced after fish has been cooked in it to make enough seasoned liquid for one or two recipes.

LOBSTER BISQUE BASE, p. 151, is a difficult preparation. Concentrated tinned or frozen creamed lobster soups, undiluted, can substitute for it. Guard against overseasoning. The soup may need to be strained or puréed. Nothing can in any way compare with lobster bisque base, but we would prefer that you use a substitute rather than dismiss the many fine recipes in which it is used.

Of the remaining basic preparations, substitutes for fresh artichoke bottoms, fresh truffles, CHERRIES IN SYRUP and PEACHES IN SYRUP are the only ones that need to be considered. The recipes in Chapter VIII indicate how to treat the tinned products if you do not use the fresh.

A few other ingredients should be mentioned. Tomato purée is quite often called for. This is a reduction of fresh tomatoes, cooked and strained, of saucelike consistency. We do not mean by this, tomato paste, a highly concentrated essence that is seldom called for. Tinned tomato purée may be used if it is not highly seasoned.

We have been careful in specifying the type of sugar required in recipes. Normally it is granulated sugar, the term used in America, the equivalent of caster sugar in Great Britain. Sometimes sugar of extra-fine grain that dissolves quickly has been suggested and sometimes confectioners' sugar (also called icing sugar in Great Britain).

We often give quite specific measurements for condiments, herbs, and spices. But we trust that any cook will know that such measurements are guides and that one should always season with caution and to taste. It is best to underseason at first and to adjust the seasoning later if necessary.

We have not mentioned one kitchen utensil that we use frequently, the *bain marie*, the authentic version of which is not likely to be found in a home kitchen. Instead, we have suggested a double boiler or double saucepan, which serves the same purpose of keeping sauces warm over warm water, away from direct heat.

Fine quality in all ingredients is naturally of first importance at all times. One must use judgment in this, however. Though usually a fresh product would be considered superior to a tinned one, the reverse may be true when the fresh product is not in season. Use good wines and liqueurs and substitute others of good quality if exactly what the recipe calls for is not available. If, for instance, Champagne is called for, it is better to use a modest but good white wine than an inferior Champagne, or to use a good wine of your own country rather than an inferior imported vintage.

THE CHOICE of a menu will be important to those of you who use our recipes to entertain. I fully realize that the days of hours-long banquets and dinner parties, with eight to fourteen courses each with carefully selected wines, are phenomena of the past. But there still are occasions for epicurean dining and on these occasions I insist on two points. One, it is quality, not quantity, that counts, and, second, there must never be repetition of any sort, either in the kind of food served or its color and texture. A well-planned meal will have each course designed to prepare the palate for the one that is to follow.

There is a formula of succession of courses that served in the old days. In its entirety, it is out of the question today, but even when a very few courses are to be served, the same order of presentation is correct. This old formula is therefore useful even if much of it is only of documentary interest.

1. HORS D'OEUVRE (Cold; Hot)
2. COLD SHELLFISH (Oysters, Clams, etc.)
3. SOUPS
4. EGGS
5. HOT FISH OR SHELLFISH
6. RELEVÉS & ENTRÉES (Sweetbreads, Poultry, Small Game, etc.)
7. MIXED ENTRÉES (Hot Vol-au-Vent, Hot Pâtés; Cold Pâtés, Galantines)
8. SHERBETS
9. PUNCH
10. SPOOMS (Wine and Fruit Juice Sherbets)
11. ROASTS (Meat, Large Game)
12. COLD ROASTS
13. VEGETABLES
14. SALADS
15. ENTREMETS (This word today means "dessert"; it originally meant a dish, sometimes a sweet or sometimes a vegetable or starch, that was served after the roast.)
16. CHEESES
17. ICES
18. CAKES
19. FRUIT
20. DESSERTS

## II

## Les Hors d'Oeuvre
*Canapés & First Courses*

## Les Soupes
*Soups*

## Les Oeufs
*Eggs*

## Les Salades
*Salads*

# Les Toasts Claude
## *Hot Liver Pâté Canapés*

To my son, who, like a good sauce, has turned out well

 ————————————

FOR THESE canapés, you may substitute some other good liver pâté or a fine liverwurst for the PLUS-QUE-PARFAIT. The truffle liquor is the liquid in which the truffles have been cooked or preserved. To serve four:

½ recipe MUSHROOM DUXELLES (p. 154)
4 slices firm white bread
Butter
6 tablespoons PLUS-QUE-PARFAIT PÂTÉ (p. 15)
4 tablespoons truffle liquor, *or* Madeira
4 tablespoons heavy cream

PREPARE half the recipe for MUSHROOM DUXELLES and keep it warm.

Trim the crusts from the bread, and fry the slices lightly in butter on each side; keep them warm.

Cream together the pâté and the truffle liquor or Madeira, and stir in the *duxelles*. Scald the cream for a few moments, stir it a little at a time into the pâté mixture, and stir just long enough to blend. The pâté should keep its consistency. Spread this on the croutons and serve immediately, as a first course.

# Les Toasts Jacques
## Hot Black Pudding Canapés

TO SERVE four:

MUSHROOM DUXELLES (p. 154)
¾ pound blood sausage
½ cup CLEAR MEAT CONSOMMÉ (p. 141), *or* substitute
4 teaspoons tomato purée *
4 teaspoons Madeira
½ cup heavy cream
4 large slices firm white bread
Butter

PREPARE the full recipe for MUSHROOM DUXELLES and keep it warm.

Discard the skin of the sausage, and mix with the sausage enough consommé to make a smooth purée. Heat this in a small saucepan, then add the tomato purée, the Madeira, the cream, and finally the *duxelles*. Stir gently and taste for seasoning.

Trim the crusts from the bread. Fry the slices lightly in butter, on each side, then spread them with the sausage mixture. Serve very hot on individual plates, as a first course.

* See p. 6 concerning tomato purée.

# Les Toasts Renouveau
## *Seafood Canapés*

To Queen Elizabeth II of England, whose charm and affectionate understanding have conquered all hearts in her vast Empire

 ———————————

To SERVE four:

4 slices white bread
6 tablespoons unsalted butter, in all
Juice of ¼ lemon
6 large boneless skinless sardines
3 tablespoons LOBSTER BISQUE BASE (p. 151)
Salt and pepper

TRIM the crusts from the bread and cut it into small diamond shapes or strips. Fry these lightly on each side in butter and cool.

Mash and blend together 4 teaspoons of the butter and the sardines. Season with lemon juice, salt, and pepper. In another bowl, blend the LOBSTER BISQUE BASE (if necessary, use undiluted tinned or frozen lobster soup) with the remaining butter until it forms a smooth paste.

Spread the fried croutons with an even layer of the sardine mixture. Using a pastry bag fitted with a small fluted tip, pipe a line of the lobster butter around the edge of each canapé. Arrange on a small serving platter and chill a short while before serving with *apéritifs* or cocktails.

## Les Baisers d'Adolphe
*Liver Pâté Pastries*

PEOPLE OFTEN ask us about the sources of our culinary titles. This delicious creation was named to keep alive the memory of a gracious tradition.

Until comparatively recently, on the occasion of the national holiday of Belgium a great and wonderful parade was held in the city of Brussels. It was a fine spectacle called the *Ommegang*. There were chariots and floats depicting allegorical and historical events and each one was surrounded by members of one of the local societies—the archers, the crossbowmen, the gymnasts, the actors, the charitable organizations, and so on. One might see the Good Giants of Brussels marching by, with St. Michael and his redoubtable Dragon, the Four Aymond Sons, and many more. They all marched through the wide streets of the city with trumpets flourishing.

At the end of the parade route, all the participants lined up in the Grand' Place, facing our beautiful town hall, and then marched in review before our well-loved mayor, Adolphe Max, who stood surrounded by his aldermen. It was then the custom for a friendly innkeeper to provide the mayor with a glass of wine offered by a lovely girl. Custom further demanded that the mayor kiss with hearty enthusiasm this ambassadress of good will. All these ceremonies were accompanied by a stirring rendition of the *Brabançonne*, the national anthem of Belgium, and by the cheering of the crowd.

*Les Baisers d'Adolphe* were named to commemorate this cheerful ritual. These little delicacies are composed of two parts, PÂTÉ PLUS-QUE-PARFAIT and PUFF PASTRY.

The day before serving them, prepare both the pâté and the pastry (see the two following recipes). If need be, substitute the finest available commercial pâté. Before assembling the pastries, have a lightly beaten egg white and a lightly beaten whole egg at hand.

Roll out some of the pastry dough into a thin sheet, and cut it with a 3-inch cooky cutter. Paint the edges of each circle with the egg white, and place a small dab of pâté on one half. Fold the other half over, like a turnover, and seal the edges by pressing them with your fingers. Brush the tops with the beaten egg, and place the pastries on lightly buttered baking sheets. Bake 20–25 minutes in a 400° F. oven, or until the pastry is well puffed and golden brown. These should be served hot from the oven, but they can be reheated if necessary.

## Pâté Plus-que-Parfait

To the dear memory of Mrs. Stephanie Chandler, Officer of the Academy, who patiently and intelligently helped me with the preparation of this book

½ pound poultry livers (chicken, turkey, squab, but never duck)
Madeira *or* Port for marinating
Brandy for marinating

2 tablespoons fine lard
6 slices streaky bacon, finely diced
1 shallot, minced
1 sprig fresh thyme
1 bay leaf
1 teaspoon brandy
2 tablespoons each sherry, Madeira, and Port
Dash of kirsch
6 tablespoons heavy cream (optional)
Salt and pepper
2 ounces truffles, minced

PLACE the livers, from which all traces of gall have been removed, in a glass or ceramic bowl and marinate them for 1½ hours in a little Port or Madeira to which a dash of brandy has been added. Turn occasionally.

Drain the livers. Heat the lard in a small skillet and, when it is very hot, sauté the livers in it briefly, just long enough to brown them on all sides.

At the same time cook the combined diced bacon, minced shallot, thyme, and bay leaf in another skillet over low heat. When the mixture begins to bubble, add the semicooked livers. Increase the heat and finish cooking the livers.

Put the mixture in a mortar or wooden bowl, and remove the thyme and bay leaf. Pound the mixture to a paste, then put it through a fine sieve. (Or, if you prefer, put it through a meat grinder twice; or purée it in an electric blender. In either case, sieve it as well. ED.)

Measure and combine the brandy, sherry, Madeira, Port, and kirsch. Add this to the pâté and mix well. Add the truffles, and season carefully with salt and freshly ground black pepper. For extra richness and flavor, add the heavy cream; this addition is optional. Cover the pâté and let it stand in a cool place to mellow for half a day.

This pâté may be presented in individual servings by packing it into little ceramic jars or *terrines*. Cover each one with buttered paper and chill them in the refrigerator. Or, it may be packed in a larger container and served as an hors d'oeuvre, at table or with cocktails, with toast or rusks. Its other purpose in our restaurant is in making sauces as well as LES BAISERS D'ADOLPHE. The quantity given here is enough for about two dozen of these little pastries, or for four to six individual *terrines*.

## How to Make Puff Pastry

THE PREPARATION of puff pastry, or *pâte feuil-letée,* demands time and some experience. For the faint-hearted, it may be wise to buy it frozen or order it from a professional baker. But it *is* possible to make it and in many places the only way to have it at all is to make it yourself. Allow plenty of time to make it properly.*

2 pounds unsalted butter
8 cups flour
1 tablespoon salt
2¼ cups ice water, approximately
Extra flour for the working surface

KNEED the butter in a bowl of ice water until it is smooth and pliable, then drain it and knead it on a marble or other working surface until all the air bubbles have been removed.

* Puff pastry succeeds best when it is made in large quantities such as in this recipe, but it is quite possible to halve the recipe. The dough can remain in the refrigerator for several days before the final rolling out, and it can also be frozen. ED.

Roll it very lightly on a floured surface to coat it on all sides, and place the resulting ball in the refrigerator to harden slightly. It is essential that the butter and the flour-water mixture that is made next be of the same firmness.

Heap the flour in the center of the working surface and fashion a well in the center with your fingertips. Put the salt in the well, and start adding the ice water very slowly with one hand while working the flour and water together with the fingertips of your other hand. Work as quickly and as lightly as possible until all the flour and enough water have been combined to make a firm (but not dry) ball. Let this stand for 30 minutes. If the weather is hot, put it in the refrigerator.

Roll the flour ball into a 12- by 14-inch rectangle with a chilled and lightly floured rolling pin. The dough should be an even ½ inch thick all over. Flatten the butter into a ½-inch-thick rectangle and place it in the center of the dough. Fold the ends and the sides of the dough toward the center to envelop the butter completely. Let this rest in a cool place for 15 minutes.

Sprinkle the working surface again very lightly with flour. Roll out the dough to a long rectangle about 21 inches long, 6 or 7 inches wide, and an even ½ inch thick throughout; the butter should not come through the flour, and it is important never to roll the pin over the edges at either end.

Fold the farther third of the rectangle back over the center third, and fold the nearer third over both layers, forming a three-layered square. Let it rest for 20 minutes, again in a cool place.

Turn the square around and roll it out on the floured surface in the opposite direction from the first rolling or *tour*, making another rectangle again 21 inches long. Fold it again as before. Rest the dough again for 20 minutes. Repeat the process twice more, flouring the working surface lightly between each *tour*. Chill the dough for 20 minutes—or as long as you like—before rolling it out for baking.

# Les Harengs à la Sauce de l'Oncle
## *Pickled Herring in Sauce*

The sauce for this dish is dedicated to our uncle, René Beaufays, who has shared in the running of our restaurant ever since I became responsible for it

PICKLED herring fillets are used for this dish. The fillets are pickled in white wine and vinegar with onion rings, carrots, herbs, and peppercorns. They are found in jars in many fine food stores. This dish makes an excellent first course. To serve four:

12 pickled herring fillets
¾ cup pickle juice
6 tablespoons dry white wine
¾ cup catsup
3 tablespoons salad oil
2 teaspoons sugar
4 teaspoons French mustard
Freshly ground black pepper

DRAIN the herring fillets, reserving the juice and the onion rings. Arrange the fillets in a shallow serving bowl. Combine the juice with the remaining ingredients and pour over the fillets. Garnish with the onion rings and sprinkle with pepper. This may be served immediately since it is not necessary for the herring to marinate in the sauce.

# Le Homard Renésauce
## *Lobster Salad*

This recipe honors a dear friend, René Mouchart, who has stood by us faithfully through good times and bad

TO SERVE four or two:

Two 1- to 1½-pound lobsters
6 tablespoons mayonnaise
2 teaspoons Worcestershire Sauce
2 tablespoons catsup
2 teaspoons minced fresh tarragon
2 teaspoons brandy
Salt and pepper
Lettuce
Buttered toast

COOK the lobster according to directions on page 62, and let it cool in its *court-bouillon*. Crack the claws, split the body down the center, and remove the meat. Dice the lobster meat, then crush it with a fork until it is quite finely shredded.

Add the remaining ingredients and mix thoroughly. Serve the lobster as an hors d'oeuvre in lettuce-lined stemmed glassware, or as a fish course in individual bowls. It should be eaten with buttered toast. Serves four or two.

# Les Tomates sans Nom
*Tomato and Shrimp Salad*

To serve four:

3–4 tomatoes
3 tablespoons olive oil
1 tablespoon lemon juice
Salt and pepper
1 tablespoon mixed minced fresh herbs (chervil,
   tarragon, parsley)
1 teaspoon minced scallion
6–8 ounces very small cooked shrimp

Choose fine ripe tomatoes. Plunge them into boiling water
for a few seconds and slip off their skins. Halve them, press
out the seeds, and cut the halves into large pieces. Put the
tomatoes in a ceramic bowl and dress them with the olive
oil, lemon juice, and a little salt and pepper. Add the herbs,
the minced scallion, and the shrimp, shelled and cleaned.
Mix together gently, let the salad marinate at room temperature for half an hour, then chill well. Serve in a glass or
crystal bowl.

# Les Céleris Tonton
## *Stuffed Celery*

THIS is a delicious hors d'oeuvre that can be served with *apéritifs* or cocktails or as an appetizer *à table*. There are two stuffings, each equally good. The quantities are for 15 to 20 pieces of celery.

*First stuffing:*

¼ pound Cheddar cheese, grated
¼ pound soft unsalted butter
1 teaspoon prepared mustard
1 teaspoon catsup
Dash of cayenne pepper

*Second stuffing:*

¼ pound Roquefort cheese
¼ pound soft unsalted butter
1 teaspoon Worcestershire Sauce

CHOOSE CRISP white pieces of celery from the heart. Wash and trim them carefully, leaving on a little of the leaves so that they can be held by one end. If you wish, mince the very tender pieces at the center that are too small to hold stuffing, and add them to either mixture. Combine the ingredients of either recipe in a small bowl, blending them thoroughly. Fill the pieces of celery and arrange them prettily on a serving platter.

# Les Céleris Anita
## *Cold Braised Celery with Anchovies*

In homage to Mrs. Anita Lloyd, a faithful friend for fifty years

FOR four to six servings:

6–8 celery hearts
Salt
Freshly ground pepper
2 tablespoons butter, approximately
2 cups hot CLEAR MEAT CONSOMMÉ (p. 141), approximately, *or* substitute
One 3-ounce can anchovy fillets
Chopped parsley
2 hard-cooked eggs

CHOOSE CRISP white celery hearts; trim and wash them well. Blanch in boiling salted water for 10 minutes, drain, and plunge into cold water; drain again and dry on a dish towel. Season the celery hearts with salt and freshly ground pepper, spreading the branches carefully to season them on the inside.

Butter a heavy, not too large casserole. Tie the celery hearts together in bundles of two or three with kitchen twine, and arrange them in one layer in the casserole. Place over a moderate flame and heat for 2 or 3 minutes. Then cover the celery with the hot consommé, put the lid on the casserole, and bake in a 300° F. oven for 1½ hours. Drain and cool.

Cut the celery hearts in two lengthwise and arrange them on a serving platter. Lay strips of anchovies on the celery, sprinkle with chopped parsley, and sieve the hard-cooked eggs over all.

## Les Escargots à la Narbonnaise
### Snails with Walnuts

This recipe is dedicated to General "Nuts" McAuliffe to celebrate the trenchant answer he gave to the challenge of his enemies in the Belgian Battle of the Ardennes in 1945

THESE snails are served in scallop shells or individual ramekins. In your country it is not likely that you will have freshly cooked snails, but if you do, discard their shells. To serve two:

12–16 large cooked or canned snails
2 strips lean bacon (⅛ inch thick)
1 tablespoon butter
½ clove garlic
1 large shallot
2 medium-size tomatoes
4 shelled and peeled walnuts
2 teaspoons MEAT JELLY (p. 145), *or* substitute
⅜ cup dry white wine
Salt and pepper
Fine dry bread crumbs

DICE THE bacon finely. Mince the garlic and shallot. Plunge the tomatoes into boiling water for a few seconds, then peel, seed, and chop them. The skins of the walnut meats are also easily removed if you first plunge them into boiling water; mince the nuts.

In a small saucepan place the diced bacon, butter, and minced garlic and shallot. (Substitute a teaspoon of minced onion if the shallot is not available.) Cook over low heat until the shallot is soft. Then add the tomatoes and nuts,

the MEAT JELLY, or substitute, the white wine, and lastly
the snails. Season lightly to taste with salt and pepper. Simmer all together until the liquid has been reduced to about
two thirds of its original volume. The sauce should not be
too thick.

Fill two scallop shells with the snails and their sauce.
Sprinkle them with the bread crumbs and brown them in
a preheated 375° F. oven. As soon as the sauce bubbles, place
the shells on individual plates, garnish with a sprig of fresh
parsley, and serve immediately.

## Les Escargots Célérité
### *Snails in Cream*

THESE snails are served not in their own shells
but in ramekins. To serve two:

12–16 large cooked or canned snails
1 celery heart
2 tablespoons butter
3 tablespoons dry sherry
¾ cup heavy cream
4 teaspoons MEAT JELLY (p. 145), *or* substitute
Salt and freshly ground pepper

SEPARATE the stalks of the celery heart, wash them thoroughly, and discard any leaves; mince very finely. Sauté
the celery in the butter over a low flame until it is almost
tender. Then increase the heat and add the sherry. Heat

25

well, and add the snails, cream, and MEAT JELLY, or substitute. Season to taste with a little salt and freshly ground
black pepper. Mix well, and cook all together over high
heat until the sauce thickens slightly; this is a matter of
moments. Serve very hot in small ramekins, with French
bread or toast.

# Le Pamplemousse Global Zobel
## *Chilled Grapefruit with Ham*

IT IS our custom to serve this grapefruit in a bowl
of crushed ice. The ingredients are:

1 small grapefruit
Salt and pepper
Minced cooked ham
Sherry or dry vermouth

SLICE off the stem end of the grapefruit, about a quarter of the
way down, and reserve it to use as a lid. With a thin sharp
knife, cut perpendicularly all around the edge of the pulp
to free it from the skin; be careful not to pierce the grapefruit shell. Then cut out each section, remove the seeds,
and remove all the white filaments in the shell. Be sure to

catch all the juice, and return it with the fruit to the shell. If there is not enough fruit to fill it, you may have to use a few pieces from a second grapefruit. Now sprinkle the grapefruit with a little salt and pepper, a spoonful of finely minced cooked ham, and a spoonful of sherry or dry vermouth. Cover with the lid and chill before serving.

## Le Consommé aux Cerises
### *Cherry Consommé*

To Madame J. Pilet, to whom we wish to pay special homage.

To SERVE two:

2 tablespoons CHERRY SYRUP (p. 158)
8–10 sour cherries (cooked or canned, p. 158)
2 teaspoons sherry
2 cups CLEAR MEAT CONSOMMÉ (p. 141)

*To serve hot:* Mix the cherries, cherry syrup, and sherry in heated soup plates. Pour the consommé, boiling hot, over the mixture, and add freshly ground pepper if desired.

*To serve cold:* Mix the ingredients well in advance and chill in the refrigerator. This may be served as jellied consommé or, if you prefer, the consommé may be diluted a little to prevent jelling.

If the cherry syrup is too thick to mix well, dilute it first with water or sherry.

27

# La Soupe à l'Oignon
## Onion Soup

ALTHOUGH onion soup is a classic recipe known to every good restaurateur, we include it here because our version is a particular favorite with many of our patrons. It is a delicious soup for a variety of occasions and very helpful for those who have spent the night devoting themselves a bit too much to "rosy Bacchus." Served in generous portions, a good onion soup is an excellent restorative. To serve two to four:

4 large white onions
Unsalted butter
4–5 cups hot CLEAR MEAT CONSOMMÉ (p. 141)
French bread or rolls
Grated Swiss cheese (Gruyère or Emmenthaler)

PEEL the onions and slice them very thin. Heat a good lump of butter in a heavy saucepan or in a casserole from which the soup can be served. Sauté the onions in this until they are golden brown but do not let them burn. Stir them frequently.

Meanwhile, spread with butter 2 or 3 slices of French bread per serving, and sprinkle them with a thick coating of grated cheese. Place them on a baking sheet and brown in a 400° F. oven.

Add the hot consommé to the onions, and pour the soup into a hot tureen if you are not serving it from the pot in which it was made. Add the toasted bread, cheese side up, and place the tureen in the oven for a few minutes. Serve immediately into heated soup bowls.

An alternate way of serving onion soup is to place a freshly poached egg in each soup bowl before pouring in the hot soup. If the soup is presented this way, the grated cheese and toasted bread are served separately.

# La Bisque de Homard
*Lobster Bisque*

To SERVE the several purposes that it does in our cooking, LOBSTER BISQUE BASE is made quite thick and concentrated, as you can see in the basic recipe on page 151. When making this choice soup, the base is simply diluted with more of the liquid ingredients of the base, that is, CONCENTRATED FISH STOCK, or CLEAR MEAT CONSOMMÉ, and cream. To serve two or three:

1 cup CONCENTRATED FISH STOCK (p. 150), *or*
    CLEAR MEAT CONSOMMÉ (p. 141)
1 cup LOBSTER BISQUE BASE (p. 151)
½ cup heavy cream
1 tablespoon brandy
1 teaspoon butter
Freshly ground pepper
2 teaspoons minced cooked lobster meat

COMBINE the fish stock (or consommé), bisque base, and cream. Boil the mixture over moderate heat until it begins to thicken again, stirring constantly with a wire whisk. This will take 5 to 10 minutes. Add the brandy and butter and a little freshly ground black pepper, and serve immediately, garnished with small pieces of lobster meat.

29

# La Savour de Nostre Mare
## *Rich Fish Soup*

Dedicated to the memory of the Reverend Petit

THIS excellent soup so frequently and easily made in our restaurant kitchen, where the *fonds de cuisine* are always on hand, is perfectly possible in home kitchens even if certain substitutions have to be made. Made in this quantity, it will serve as an excellent beginning to a large buffet supper or dinner party. To serve twelve to sixteen:

2 pounds mussels in their shells
2 pounds various small fish (smelts, whitebait, sole, butterfish, etc.)
One 1¼-pound lobster
¼ pound shrimp
COURT-BOUILLON (p. 149)
4 cups CONCENTRATED FISH STOCK (p. 150)
2 cups LOBSTER BISQUE BASE (p. 151)
8 cups CLEAR MEAT CONSOMMÉ (p. 141)
2 cups heavy cream
Pinch of saffron
1 clove of garlic, minced
Salt and pepper

COOK the mussels according to directions on page 47. Remove them from their shells and trim off the "beards." Ladle the cooking liquid into a large saucepan or into a deep serving casserole. Take care not to let any sand that may have settled in the bottom of the pan be included in the broth. Put the trimmed mussels in the clear broth.

Follow directions on page 149 for making the *court-bouillon* and poaching the fish, which should be cleaned, boned, and cut into rather large pieces if necessary. Remove the cooked fish from the *court-bouillon* with a slotted spoon. In the same stock boil the lobster for 15 to 20 minutes. Remove the lobster, and put in the shrimp, which have been previously cleaned and shelled; simmer 5 minutes.

Put the fish and the shelled lobster and shrimp in the mussel broth, and add the CONCENTRATED FISH STOCK. However, an excellent substitute for this is, of course, the strained *court-bouillon* in which the fish and shellfish have just been cooked. Add the LOBSTER BISQUE BASE or, lacking that, an equal quantity of undiluted tinned or frozen lobster soup. Add the consommé, or an equal amount of the best tinned variety available. Add the cream, saffron, and the freshly ground pepper. Salt to taste; there may be no need of extra salt. Let the soup simmer until it begins to thicken, and serve it in heated soup plates.

## Les Oeufs Brouillés à l'Armoricaine
### *Scrambled Eggs with Lobster, Cream and Brandy*

TO SERVE two:

½ cup LOBSTER BISQUE BASE (p. 151)
2 tablespoons diced lobster meat
¾ cup heavy cream, in all
2 teaspoons brandy
4–6 eggs
2 tablespoons butter
Salt and pepper

UNDILUTED frozen or tinned lobster soup can substitute for both the LOBSTER BISQUE BASE and the diced lobster.

Heat together the bisque base, the lobster meat, 3 tablespoons of heavy cream, and the brandy, over low heat, until the mixture thickens slightly. At the same time, combine the eggs, the rest of the cream, and the butter in a heavy saucepan. Season with salt and pepper, and cook over a low heat, whisking constantly, until the eggs are thick and creamy.

Serve the eggs in a small serving dish with some of the sauce poured over them. Serve the rest of the sauce in a sauceboat.

# L'Omelette Tricolore
## Omelette with Truffles and Madeira

In homage to the Soldier King, Albert I

TO SERVE TWO:

2–3 tomatoes
Butter
Salt and pepper
4 teaspoons diced truffles
4 teaspoons MEAT JELLY (p. 145), *or* substitute
6 tablespoons Madeira
3–4 eggs

PLUNGE the tomatoes into boiling water for a few seconds, peel them, halve them, and press out the seeds. Cut them into large pieces, and heat them slowly in a small saucepan with a lump of butter. Season with salt and pepper.

In another saucepan, heat the truffles with the MEAT JELLY, or substitute, and the Madeira. At the same time, beat the eggs lightly and make an omelette in the usual manner. Just before folding it, put in the tomatoes. Slip the omelette onto a warm serving platter, cover with the truffle sauce, and serve immediately.

## La Salade Crésus
*Beans, Artichoke, and Asparagus with Grapes*

FOR four to six servings:

1 bunch white grapes
½ pound very small fresh green beans
8 small artichoke bottoms ( p. 154)
1 pound asparagus
Juice of 1 lemon
¾ cup heavy cream
2 tablespoons catsup
Salt and pepper

PEEL the grapes if the skins are tough. Keep them cool.

Wash the beans and snap off the ends, removing any strings. Boil the beans in salted water until they are just tender; drain and rinse immediately under cold running water. The beans must have a crunchy texture.

If you are using fresh artichokes, cook them according to the basic recipe, and remove the leaves and chokes; or you may use tinned ones.

Wash the asparagus thoroughly, tie the stalks in bundles of three or four, and cook them in plenty of boiling salted water (2 teaspoons of salt to a quart of water). Drain them and cut off the tender tips to use in the salad.*

\* Fine Belgian white asparagus, cooked and packed in jars, are exported to all parts of the world; they are ideal for this salad. ED.

Arrange the beans and asparagus in bouquets in a handsome salad bowl, garnish with the artichoke bottoms and grapes, and keep cool until servingtime.

Mix together well the lemon juice, cream, and catsup. Season this dressing with salt and freshly ground pepper, and pour it over the salad before serving. You may wish to make a larger quantity of dressing in order also to serve some in a sauceboat.

## La Salade Idéale
*Green Salad with Cream and Lemon Juice Dressing*

 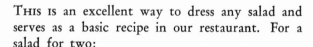

THIS IS an excellent way to dress any salad and serves as a basic recipe in our restaurant. For a salad for two:

Salad greens, endive, tomatoes, etc.
Juice of ½ lemon

3 tablespoons olive oil
6 tablespoons heavy cream
1 teaspoon tomato catsup
1 teaspoon prepared mustard
1 small onion, minced
1 teaspoon chopped parsley
Pinch of chopped tarragon
Salt and pepper to taste

WASH and dry the salad greens well and tear them into serving pieces. Tomatoes should be peeled, seeded, and cut into wedges. Mix the ingredients for the dressing in a small bowl or pitcher, and mix well again before using. Pour the dressing over the salad and toss just before serving. Serve in a glass or pottery bowl.

## La Salade Ysaÿe
### *Pear Salad with Celeriac*

Dedicated to the memory of a great Belgian musician

TO SERVE four:

4 firm pears
1½ cups water
1½ cups sugar
Vanilla bean
1 celery root (celeriac)
Juice of 1 lemon

6 tablespoons salad oil
2 small onions
2 teaspoons minced fresh tarragon
Pinch of cinnamon
Salt and pepper

PREPARE a syrup of equal parts of sugar and water. Add a piece of vanilla bean, and bring to a boil, stirring frequently. Reduce the heat and add the pears, first peeled, halved, and cored. Poach them until they are just tender, then remove and let them cool.

Peel and quarter the celery root and cut it into fine julienne strips. Parboil these for 1 minute in rapidly boiling salted water. Drain, season with salt and pepper, and cool. If celery root is not available, substitute finely diced celery hearts.

In a small bowl combine the lemon juice, salad oil, the onions, finely chopped, the minced tarragon, and the cinnamon, salt, and freshly ground pepper. Mix well. Arrange the pears and celery in a glass or china bowl, pour the dressing over them, and serve chilled.

La Sauce Chantraine

La Sauce Secret de Tante Félicie

La Sauce Crémaillère

*Three Important Sauces*
*Created at the Restaurant Chantraine*

# La Sauce Chantraine

In memory of my father, who so often gave us the example of tranquil courage

 ————————————————

THIS IS our restaurant's oldest original recipe. It is not only delicious, it is also exceptionally adaptable, as it accompanies with equal success such varied foods as veal, beef, chicken, sweetbreads, kidneys, artichokes, truffles, hare, pheasant, partridge, woodcock, and young boar.

Making the sauce presents no difficulty, although I must warn you about a few things. If you are obliged to use a commercial substitute for MEAT JELLY, take care not to oversalt. If the sauce turns, this means there is too much fat; to rectify this, add one or two spoonfuls of cold water. The sauce is always prepared in the pan in which the food it is to accompany has been cooked. The food will have been cooked in butter. It is important, therefore, that every bit of this butter be removed before the sauce is started. (The discarded butter can be used for frying the toast strips or triangles that usually garnish these dishes.)

Basically, the preparation of the sauce is the same for all foods, but I will indicate certain differences. In our restaurant, the amount prescribed in the recipe is served for two or three but you may find it sufficient for four to six people.

⅜ cup brandy
1¾ cups heavy cream
3½ tablespoons MEAT JELLY (p. 145), *or* substitute
1 tablespoon prepared mustard
Thinly sliced white bread

### *Sauce Chantraine for Meat, Fowl, Game:*

SAUTÉ the meat (such as chicken breasts, cutlets of veal, a piece of filet of beef or game) in sufficient butter until it is brown on all sides but not thoroughly cooked. Remove the meat to a cutting board, and pour off *all* the butter into another pan. Cut the meat into serving pieces as necessary, and return it to the first pan. Place over high heat and, when the pan is thoroughly heated, add the brandy. Touch it with a lighted match, and shake the pan until the flames have subsided. Then add the cream, MEAT JELLY, and mustard. Stir well, reduce the heat, and let the sauce cook gently with the meat until the sauce thickens. Taste for seasoning. Serve on a heated platter or, if you prefer, this can all be done in a flameproof serving dish that can be brought to the table. Garnish with strips or triangles of toast sautéed in the butter in which the meat was first cooked.

### *Sauce Chantraine for Sweetbreads:*

COOK the sweetbreads according to the directions on page 93. Cut them into serving pieces, and gently reheat them in butter in a covered saucepan over a low flame. When they are thoroughly heated, pour off all the butter, and make the sauce as above, always over moderate heat.

To add mushrooms, artichoke bottoms, or truffles to sauce Chantraine:

### *Sauce Chantraine with Mushrooms:*

WHEN MUSHROOMS are to be added to sauce Chantraine, usually in the case of a meat, sweetbread, kidney, or chicken dish, the mushrooms are cooked in advance (see page 153). The sauce is started without the mushrooms in the pan, for they must not be cooked again. Only when the sauce begins to thicken are the mushrooms added, with some of their cooking liquor for added flavor, and they are merely heated in the sauce.

### *Sauce Chantraine with Artichokes or Truffles:*

PLACE PREVIOUSLY cooked artichoke bottoms (see page 154) or truffles (see page 155) in a saucepan with butter. In the case of artichokes, add a spoonful of Madeira; in the case of truffles, add a spoonful of Madeira and Port combined. Heat gently, covered, over a moderate flame, then pour off all the butter (which will be delicious for sautéing a toast garnish), and proceed as for sauce Chantraine for meat.

# La Sauce Secret de Tante Félicie
## Sorrel Sauce

To those splendid authors and artists, Mr. and Mrs. Fred Funcken

THIS unusual sauce is easy to make and is exquisite served with veal, chicken, sweetbreads, or any white meat. The following proportions are for four to six servings.

½ pound fresh sorrel
Butter
⅜ cup Port or Madeira
4 teaspoons MEAT JELLY (p. 145), *or* substitute
1¾ cups heavy cream
Salt and pepper

PICK over the sorrel and wash it carefully. Chop it fine, and heat it in a saucepan with a lump of butter. Simmer until the sorrel is tender and the liquid has evaporated. (If fresh sorrel is not available, use tinned sorrel which, however, is usually puréed. Use 4 tablespoons or more to taste. ED.)

Sauté the chosen meat in butter until it is nearly done. Remove the meat to a cutting board, and pour off *all* the butter from the pan. Cut the meat into serving portions, and return it to the pan. Reheat the pan, add the wine, and cook for a moment. Then add the MEAT JELLY, the cooked sorrel, and the cream. Stir well, season with salt and pepper, and cook until the sauce thickens. Serve on a heated platter, garnished with triangles or strips of bread sautéed in the butter in which the meat was cooked.

# La Sauce Crémaillère
## *Hollandaise for Fish or Lobster*

THIS IS an exquisite sauce that can be served with almost every kind of fish (sole, turbot, trout, halibut, brill, etc.) as well as with lobster and *langoustes* (spiny or rock lobster). Fish and crustaceans are handled slightly differently, as is indicated below. The sauce cannot be reheated—it would curdle immediately if it were—so it must be made shortly before serving.

*To serve with fish:*

POACH THE fish (see page 50) in COURT-BOUILLON (page 149). However, instead of slicing the vegetables for the *court-bouillon,* dice them very finely before cooking them in the butter (this is called a *brunoise*).

Make a MOUSSELINE SAUCE (see the following recipe), using only *½ tablespoon of water* and *adding 1 tablespoon of lemon juice.* Keep it warm in a double boiler when it is done.

When the fish is cooked, arrange it, first well drained, on a platter and keep it warm. Strain the *court-bouillon.* Keep the vegetables, but remove from them the sprigs of thyme and parsley, the bay leaf, cloves, and peppercorns. Stir the well-drained vegetables into the sauce with a whisk and mix vigorously. Pour the sauce over the fish and serve immediately.

*To serve with lobster:*

LOBSTER MAY also be cooked in *court-bouillon* (see page 62). As in the preceding recipe for fish, the vegetables must be finely diced.

43

Let the lobster drain a few minutes when it is done, and strain the *court-bouillon* and reserve the vegetables as before. Detach the claws and joints of the lobster, crack them (the joints may be cut with strong scissors), and remove all the meat. Lay the lobster on its back on a board and, with a strong knife, split it lengthwise from head to tail. Remove all the meat and cut it into large serving pieces. Unlike fish, the lobster meat is now kept warm and moist in the strained *court-bouillon*.

The sauce is now prepared exactly as it is for fish. When it is ready, drain the lobster meat well, arrange it on a hot platter, pour the sauce over it, and serve immediately.

## How to Prepare Sauce Mousseline

To SERVE four or more:

½ pound unsalted butter
3 egg yolks
1 tablespoon water
Salt and pepper

MELT THE butter in a saucepan and keep it lukewarm. In a very heavy saucepan (or in the top of a double boiler), beat together the egg yolks and water with a whisk. Season with salt and pepper. Cook the yolks over a very low heat (or barely simmering water) until they begin to thicken noticeably. Now pour in bit by bit the lukewarm melted butter, stirring fast and constantly. If the sauce thickens too much, thin it cautiously with small spoonfuls of cold water. Taste again for seasoning, and keep the sauce over warm water until you are ready to serve it. In our restaurant, *sauce mousseline* is served particularly with sole.

# IV

## Les Moules en Coquilles
*Mussels in Scallop Shells*

## Les Soles
*Sole*

## Les Truites
*Trout*

## Les Homards
*Lobster*

## How to Cook Mussels

THIS recipe is primarily intended as a preliminary step in preparing mussels for other dishes. However, once cooked in this manner, the mussels may be served, in their shells, in soup dishes. Ladle the broth from the top to avoid particles of sand, and pour it over the mussels. Season the broth lightly with salt and pepper if necessary.

TO SERVE two or more:

4 quarts mussels in their shells
3 tablespoons butter, melted
2 shallots, minced
1 stalk of celery, thinly sliced
1 sprig of thyme
1 bay leaf
Freshly ground black pepper
1½ cups dry white wine

SCRAPE the "beards" from the mussels, using a sharp sturdy knife. Scrub and wash the mussels in several changes of cold water.

Place the mussels and all the other ingredients in a kettle. Cover the kettle and cook over high heat until the mussels open. Discard any that are reluctant to open. Take the mussels out of the kettle and put them in a colander, leaving the broth to settle a little before serving.

To use the mussels in other dishes, remove them from their shells and discard any filaments clinging to them from inside the rims of the shells.

## La Coquille Rayca
### *Gratinéed Mussels in Scallop Shells*

THOUGH this dish should be served in scallop shells, ramekins make good substitutes. To fill four shells:

4 quarts mussels
DUCHESSE POTATOES (p. 156)
3 tablespoons butter, in all
2½ tablespoons flour
1¼ cups broth from the mussels
½ clove of garlic
2 teaspoons minced parsley
2 egg yolks
Grated Swiss cheese

FOLLOW the directions on page 47 for cooking and shelling mussels. Meanwhile, boil and mash the potatoes for the POTATOES DUCHESSE. When the mussels are done, strain the broth and let it rest for a while away from the fire. Measure out the amount of broth specified for the sauce, and reduce it slightly over moderate heat.

Make a very light *roux:* Melt two thirds of the butter in a heavy saucepan, stir the flour into it, and cook over low heat, stirring constantly, until the mixture colors lightly. Set it aside to cool.

In another saucepan, cook the garlic in the remaining butter but do not let it brown. Add the reduced mussel broth and simmer together for a few moments. Meanwhile, finish the potatoes and put the purée in a pastry bag with a fluted tip.

Remove the garlic from the simmering broth, and stir

48

the broth into the butter-flour *roux*. Stir over moderate heat until the sauce is well blended, then add the mussels and parsley. Simmer all together for 5 minutes. Then mix in the egg yolks, one at a time, stirring vigorously, and remove the pan immediately from the fire.

Fill the shells or ramekins with the sauced mussels, sprinkle them with grated cheese, and pipe the potatoes around the edges of the shells. Brown them in a hot (450° F.) oven for a few minutes, and serve immediately.

## La Coquille Hans Pettersson
### *Mussels with Shrimp and Mushrooms in Scallop Shells*

In homage to the illustrious scholar, Hans Pettersson of Göteberg, whose friendship honors us and is one of the most precious gifts bestowed upon us

THIS DISH is usually served in scallop shells but individual ramekins may also be used. To fill four shells:

4 quarts mussels
¼ pound mushrooms, cooked (p.. 154)
¼ pound small shrimp, cooked, shelled, and deveined
2 shallots, minced
2 tablespoons butter
¾ cup dry white wine
¾ cup heavy cream
2 egg yolks
Salt and pepper

FOLLOW the directions on page 47 for cooking and shelling mussels. Cook the mushrooms as the basic recipe indicates; however, they should be sliced rather than left whole. Prepare the shrimp.

In a heavy saucepan, melt the butter and in it sauté the minced shallots until they are soft but not brown. Then add the white wine and the mussels, mushrooms, and shrimp. Simmer all together over low heat until only a little liquid remains in the bottom of the pan.

Meanwhile, in another saucepan, simmer the cream until it thickens. When it is almost of saucelike consistency, remove it from the fire and, with a sauce whisk, quickly beat in the egg yolks, one at a time. Add to this the mussel mixture, stir well together, and season lightly with salt and pepper. Fill the scallop shells and brown briefly in a hot (450° F.) oven.

## How to Cook Sole

THE EUROPEAN or Dover sole is one of the most delicate fish that can appear on a gourmet's table. It has no equal.* In
* The nearest American approximations are the small flounders, grey and lemon sole, dab, winter flounder, and yellowtail. The culinary preparation for these is the same as for European sole.
most markets, the whole fish will be prepared for you, or filletted, as you prefer. Whole sole are always cooked skinned.

Always cook the fish in a pan large enough for it to lie flat on the bottom. Cover it with CONCENTRATED FISH STOCK (page 150) or with COURT-BOUILLON FOR FISH (page 149). The liquid should be cool when the fish is placed in it.

Bring the liquid to a point just below the boil; it should

quiver but not actually bubble. When it is done, remove the fish to a wooden board and, with a very sharp knife, cut away the small bones all around the edge. Transfer the fish to a lightly buttered warm serving platter and keep it warm while its sauce is being prepared. Sole fillets may, of course, be cooked and served in the same manner as a whole fish.

DUCHESSE POTATOES (page 156) are a classic accompaniment to sole. If they are to be used, the potato purée should be piped around the edge of the serving platter with a pastry tube and fluted tip and browned in the oven before the fish is placed on the platter.

## La Sole S.O.N.

*Sole with White Wine Sauce, Mushrooms, and Tomatoes*

TO SERVE four:

4 small whole sole, *or* 2 pounds sole fillets
COURT-BOUILLON (p. 149)
DUCHESSE POTATOES (p. 156), optional
12 mushroom caps, cooked (p. 153)
4 small tomatoes
Butter, salt pepper
1 cup reduced *court-bouillon* (above)
2 tablespoons butter
¾ cup dry white wine
3 tablespoons dry vermouth
3–4 egg yolks,* lightly beaten

* The number of egg yolks needed to thicken this fairly light sauce will vary depending on the size of the yolks and how much the sauce is reduced before they are added. ED.

PREPARE the COURT-BOUILLON and let it cool. Include in it, if possible, the trimmings of the fish. Have the fish, ready to cook, in the refrigerator.

If you are using the DUCHESSE POTATOES, prepare them and pipe them around the edge of the platter. Brown them in the oven shortly before you finish cooking the fish.

Cook the mushrooms. Peel the tomatoes, cut them into quarters, and seed and drain them carefully. Simmer them with a good lump of butter and salt and pepper until they are tender but the pieces still keep their shapes. Keep the mushrooms and tomatoes warm, or reheat them at the last minute.

Poach the sole in the *court-bouillon* (see the instructions on page 50). When it is done, arrange it, first trimmed and well drained, on the platter (butter the platter lightly if you have just baked the potato garnish on it), and keep it warm.

Reduce the *court-bouillon* over a brisk fire until it thickens slightly. Then strain it and measure out the amount specified for the sauce. In a heavy saucepan, combine the reduced fish stock and the butter, white wine, and vermouth. Continue to boil down over high heat, stirring often, until the liquid is reduced to two thirds its original quantity. Remove from the heat and, with a sauce whisk, beat in quickly the lightly beaten egg yolks. Heat the sauce very gently now, beating constantly with the whisk, and remove from the fire as soon as it thickens.

Mask the fish on the platter with the sauce and surround it with the mushrooms and tomatoes, which must first be carefully drained. Serve immediately, and if there is extra sauce, pass it in a sauceboat.

# La Sole New York Herald Tribune
*Poached Sole with Mousseline, Vermouth, and Cream Sauce*

THIS DISH, like so many others of *haute cuisine,* is made of a combination of important basic recipes. The timing of these various elements makes the preparation a little complicated in this instance, as all the preparations, as nearly as possible, must be made simultaneously. And it is most important that all the elements be kept hot until it is time to assemble them. Though this is not a dish for beginners, anyone will find it interesting to study how this type of classic presentation is achieved. To serve four:

4 small whole sole, *or* 2 pounds sole fillets
COURT-BOUILLON (p. 149)
12 mushroom caps, cooked (p. 153)
12 small shrimp, cooked
4 teaspoons diced truffle
DUCHESSE POTATOES (p. 156)
½ cup reduced *court-bouillon* (above), *or* CON-
   CENTRATED FISH STOCK (p. 150)
⅜ cup dry vermouth
½ cup cream
1 small onion, very finely minced
SAUCE MOUSSELINE (p. 44)
Salt and pepper

PREPARE the COURT-BOUILLON and let it cool. Include in it, if possible, the trimmings of the fish. Have the fish, ready to cook, in the refrigerator.

Cook the mushrooms and shrimp, and dice the truffles.

Prepare the DUCHESSE POTATOES, and keep them warm. (The purée, to make a perfect presentation, should be piped around the edge of the platter and browned in the oven just before the fish is ready to be transferred to the platter, as described on page 51. However, it may be more convenient for the housewife to present the potatoes baked in a separate dish of their own. ED.)

Poach the sole in the *court-bouillon* (see the instructions on page 50). At the same time, in a small separate saucepan, heat the mushrooms, shrimp, and truffles in a few spoonfuls of the same *court-bouillon*. When the fish is done, arrange it, first trimmed and well drained, on a warm platter. Drain the mushrooms, shrimp, and truffles, reserving the liquid, and garnish the fish with them. Keep the platter warm, and meanwhile have ready the ingredients for the sauce that follows.

Strain the *court-bouillon,* and reduce it rapidly over high heat. (Or, you may use instead, if you have it on hand, some CONCENTRATED FISH STOCK.) Combine the specified quantities of this reduced stock and of the dry vermouth and cream, and add the very finely minced onion and the reserved liquid in which the garnishes were heated. Season lightly with salt and pepper. Simmer this sauce over a brisk flame until it is reduced to about two-thirds its original quantity; it will begin to thicken and form small bubbles when it is ready.

Meanwhile, make the SAUCE MOUSSELINE and, if it must wait, keep it warm over warm water. These two parts of the final sauce should be ready at about the same time, however. Combine the stock-vermouth-and-cream mixture and the *mousseline,* whipping well with a whisk, and reheat them together, still whipping and taking care not to let the sauce approach the boil. Pour it over the sole as soon as it is heated through, and serve immediately.

# La Sole Art Buchwald
## *Poached Sole with Mousseline and Lobster Cream Sauce*

With our sincere greetings to the celebrated chronicler

 ————————————

TO SERVE four:

4 small whole sole, *or* 2 pounds sole fillets
COURT-BOUILLON (p. 149)
A few pieces of cooked lobster
⅜ cup dry white wine
½ cup cream
½ cup LOBSTER BISQUE BASE (p. 151)\*
½ cup CONCENTRATED FISH STOCK (p. 150)
SAUCE MOUSSELINE (p. 44)

PREPARE the COURT-BOUILLON and let it cool. Include in it, if possible, the trimmings of the fish. Have the fish, ready to cook, in the refrigerator.

The cooking of the fish and of the two parts of the sauce are nearly simultaneous procedures. Poach the sole in the *court-bouillon* (see the instructions on page 50). Warm a few pieces of cooked lobster in butter or a little *court-bouillon*. When the fish is done, arrange it, first trimmed and well-drained, on a platter, garnish it with the lobster, and keep it warm.

Meanwhile, start the two sauces: Combine the white wine, cream, LOBSTER BISQUE, or a substitute, and CONCENTRATED

\* Frozen or tinned lobster soup, undiluted, can substitute, if necessary, for lobster bisque base.

FISH STOCK * in a heavy saucepan. Simmer the mixture over a moderately high flame, stirring often to prevent sticking, until it is reduced to about two-thirds its original quantity; it will begin to thicken and form small bubbles when it is ready. Keep it warm over warm water.

Make the SAUCE MOUSSELINE and, if it must wait, keep it warm also over warm water. These two parts of the final sauce should be ready at about the same time, however. Pour the lobster cream sauce into the *mousseline*, beat the sauces vigorously together with a whisk, and remove from the heat as soon as the sauce is heated through. Take care not to let it approach the boil. Pour the sauce over the fish and serve immediately.

## La Sole Baudouin
### *Poached Sole with Two Sauces*

To Baudouin, King of the Belgians, we dedicate this creation of our culinary art as a token of our admiration and respect

THIS DISH is royally inspired and royally presented. To our minds, it represents a link between the past and the present in that it offers two

---

* As in the preceding recipe for SOLE NEW YORK HERALD TRIBUNE, if you do not have concentrated fish stock on hand, you may reduce a little of the *court-bouillon* after the fish has been cooked in it, and then add it to the first three ingredients of this sauce. You may start simmering the lobster sauce before the reduced stock is ready if you wish. ED.

sauces, the classic lobster cream sauce and our own creation which we call SAUCE CRÉMAILLÈRE. It is not, of course, a simple preparation and the person making this dish should read the directions for COURT-BOUILLON and for cooking sole (page 50) and the recipes for the MOUSSELINE and CRÉMAILLÈRE sauces before beginning. But it is a dish to inspire the connoisseur. To serve four:

4 small whole sole, *or* 2 pounds sole fillets
COURT-BOUILLON (p. 149)
1 cup LOBSTER BISQUE BASE (p. 151)*
½ cup heavy cream
2 teaspoons brandy
Salt and pepper
SAUCE CRÉMAILLÈRE (p. 43)

PREPARE the COURT-BOUILLON, cutting the vegetables into small dice before sautéeing them, as prescribed in the recipe for SAUCE CRÉMAILLÈRE. Cool the *court-bouillon.*

Two double boilers are helpful to make the two sauces conveniently. In the top of one double boiler, over direct heat, combine the LOBSTER BISQUE BASE, or substitute, with the cream. Boil the mixture over a brisk flame until it begins to thicken again, stirring well and often with a whisk to prevent sticking. Toward the end of the cooking, add the brandy. Keep the sauce warm over warm water.

Poach the fish at the same time that you start the first sauce, or sooner. Do this in the *court-bouillon,* according to the directions on page 50.

As soon as possible, prepare the *mousseline* (page 44) that is the base for the *crémaillère* sauce in the top of the second double boiler. Keep the sauce warm over warm water if it must wait.

* Frozen or tinned lobster soup, undiluted, can substitute, if necessary, for lobster bisque base.

When the fish is done, remove it from its broth, drain and trim it well, and arrange it on a large hot serving platter; be sure to keep it warm. Add to the *mousseline* the lemon juice and the diced vegetables drained from the broth as the recipe for *crémaillère* sauce indicates.

With a large spoon, mask the fish with the sauces: If these are whole fish, cover half of each one lengthwise with each sauce; if you have used fillets, mask each one alternately with one sauce on one and the other sauce on the next. Do this carefully so that the two sauces remain separate, as this is the characteristic feature of the dish. Serve immediately.

# La Truite de Mon Village
### *Trout with Juniper Berries and Herb Butter*

To serve two:

2 trout
Salt and pepper
Flour
Butter
4–6 juniper berries, crushed
2 shallots, finely minced
2 teaspoons minced parsley
3 tablespoons unsalted butter
Juice of ½ lemon

CLEAN THE trout, cut off the fins, but leave on the heads and tails. Wash the fish well inside and out, pat them dry with a towel, and sprinkle them with salt, pepper, and a little flour.

In a skillet, melt enough butter to completely cover the bottom of the skillet. Add the trout when the butter is sizzling. Cook the fish, turning them once, for about 7 to 8 minutes. Shortly before they are done, add the crushed juniper berries.

Meanwhile, in a small bowl cream together the butter and the minced shallots and parsley. Add the lemon juice, season with salt and freshly ground pepper, and mix well. Serve the trout on a very hot platter and pass the seasoned butter separately.

# La Truite au Sourire de Reims
## *Poached Trout with White Wine Sauce*

THE SAUCE for this dish can be used on different sorts of delicate fish such as sole, turbot, or flounder, but it was especially designed for trout. To serve two:

2 medium trout
COURT-BOUILLON (p. 149)
1 shallot, minced
¾ cup dry white wine (preferably Champagne or Vouvray, if available)
Salt and pepper
¾ cup heavy cream
2 tablespoons tomato purée *
Pinch of chopped fresh tarragon

* See p. 6 concerning tomato purée.

CLEAN THE trout, cut off the fins, but leave on the heads and tails. Wash the fish well inside and out, and refrigerate them until you are ready to cook them.

Prepare the COURT-BOUILLON, cutting the vegetables into small dice rather than slices, as they will be used in the presentation of the dish. Let the *court-bouillon* cool. Then poach the trout in it; see the instructions for poaching on page 50. Trout, however, unlike sole, is poached with its skin on. Allow 10 to 12 minutes for a ½-pound trout.

Meanwhile, in a small heavy saucepan, heat together the minced shallot and wine; add a little salt and pepper. When the wine begins to boil, add the cream, the tomato purée, and the tarragon. Cook the sauce until it thickens, stirring occasionally. When it is of a good consistency, stir in another teaspoon of wine, beat the sauce vigorously with a whisk, and keep it warm over warm water.

When the trout are cooked, remove them from the *court-bouillon,* and skin them or not, as you prefer. Arrange them, first well drained, on a hot platter and keep them warm. Strain the *court-bouillon* through a sieve, and keep the diced vegetables but remove the sprigs of thyme and parsley, the bay leaf, and the cloves and peppercorns. Arrange the vegetables around the trout, and mask the fish with sauce. If there is extra sauce, pass it in a sauceboat.

# La Truite du Souvenir
## *Baked Trout in Cheese Soufflé Sauce*

Dedicated to the memory of a great artist, Berthe Roggen

To SERVE four:

4 trout
Milk, flour, butter
2 tablespoons butter
1 heaping tablespoon flour
1¼ cups milk
2 egg yolks
⅝ cup grated Swiss cheese
Pinch of grated nutmeg
Salt and pepper
6 egg whites

THE TROUT should be cleaned, the fins cut off, and the heads and tails left on; they should also be boned before they are cooked. You may wish to have this done for you at the fish market.

Start the sauce before you cook the trout: In a small heavy saucepan, melt the butter and stir in the flour. Stir over moderate heat for 2 or 3 minutes, and do not let the mixture brown. Then add the milk, and stir until the sauce boils. Remove from the fire, and stir in the egg yolks, one by one, stir in the cheese, season lightly with nutmeg, salt, and pepper, and set aside.

Wash the trout, dip them in milk, then dip them in a little flour, coating them lightly. In a large skillet, melt enough butter to completely cover the bottom of the skillet. When the butter is sizzling, brown the trout in it, one or two at a time, turning them once. Add more butter if necessary to cook all the trout. When they are brown, arrange them in a lightly buttered baking dish.

Meanwhile, beat the egg whites until they are stiff, and fold the egg-yolk mixture into them gently. Cover the trout with this batter, and bake them in a hot (400° F.) oven until the soufflé sauce is a lovely golden brown. Serve immediately.

## How to Cook Lobster

PREPARE the ingredients of a COURT-BOUILLON according to the recipe on page 149. For lobster, however, increase the amount of salt to 4 teaspoons and the amount of peppercorns to 3 teaspoons. You may also augment the quantity of vegetables. To cook a large lobster, or several lobsters, you will need to increase the recipe proportionately so that the lobsters will be submerged in liquid when they are cooked.

Bring the *court-bouillon* to a rapid boil in a large kettle. Plunge the lobster immediately into it and cover the kettle. Boil gently for 20 to 25 minutes for lobsters weighing 1½ to 2 pounds.

If the lobster is to be served cold, transfer it and the *court-bouillon* to a ceramic bowl, and let stand for several hours or even overnight. Never put a lobster in the refrigerator until it is thoroughly cooled.

# Le Homard Walter Scott
*Baked Stuffed Lobster*

To serve two:

One 2-pound lobster
*Court-bouillon* for lobster (p. 62)
6 mushrooms, cooked (p. 153)
3 tablespoons unsalted butter
2 onions
½ cup heavy cream
½ cup CONCENTRATED FISH STOCK (p. 150)
2 egg yolks
1 teaspoon prepared mustard
Salt and pepper
Grated Gruyère cheese

Boil the lobster in a *court-bouillon* according to the directions on page 62. Cook the mushrooms according to the basic recipe; they should, however, be sliced rather than left whole.

While the lobster is cooking, in a heavy pan, over low heat, cook the chopped onions slowly in the butter until they are very soft but not at all brown. In another pan, simmer together the cream and CONCENTRATED FISH STOCK until the mixture thickens. Then strain the butter from the onions into this sauce, and discard the onions. Bring the sauce back to the boiling point, stirring well. Now, off the fire, with a sauce whisk beat in the egg yolks, one at a time, and the mustard. Beat well until the sauce is smooth and thick. Season it very lightly with salt and pepper.

As soon as the lobster is done, remove it from the kettle. Separate the claws from the body and crack them open; cut off and split the joints with scissors. Extract all the meat. Place the lobster on its back on a wooden board, and cut it

63

lengthwise completely in two with a strong sharp knife, running it from the top of the body down through the tail. Remove the tail meat and empty the cavity of the shells.

Dice or slice all the lobster meat, fill the shells with it, add the sliced mushrooms and the hot sauce, and sprinkle with grated cheese. Brown the lobster briefly in a hot (450° F.) oven, and serve immediately.

## Le Homard Léopold
*Lobster in Cream with Brandy and Truffles*

In homage to all the Kings of the Belgians

TO SERVE TWO:

2 small lobsters
*Court-bouillon* for lobster (p. 62)
12 mushroom caps, cooked (p. 153)
4 teaspoons chopped truffles
2 teaspoons Madeira, optional
2 tablespoons butter
2 tablespoons minced shallots
3 tablespoons brandy
1 teaspoon anise liqueur
1¾ cups heavy cream
½ teaspoon curry powder
Salt and pepper

BOIL the lobster in a *court-bouillon* according to the directions on page 62. Remove it from the kettle as soon as it is done.

Drain, open, and shell the lobster as described in the preceding recipe for HOMARD WALTER SCOTT. Cut the meat into large pieces. It may then be kept moist in the *court-bouillon;* drain it well again before using.

Cook the mushrooms according to the basic recipe. If you are so fortunate as to have fresh truffles, cook them according to the directions on page 155; otherwise, dice the contents of a small tin of truffles and warm them in their own liquor, adding, if you wish, 2 teaspoons of Madeira.

In a heavy saucepan, heat together the butter and shallots, then add the pieces of lobster, the truffles, drained (reserve the liquor), and the mushrooms. Cook all together over fairly high heat, stirring often, until the lobster is heated through. Then add the brandy and anise liqueur, touch with a lighted match, and shake the pan until the flames die down. Then add the cream, the truffle liquor, the curry powder, and a little salt and pepper. Mix well and simmer gently until the sauce thickens.

Serve very hot, with boiled rice or in a RICE RING (page 157).

# Le Homard Diablotin
*Broiled Lobster with Two Sauces*

 ——————————

THIS RECIPE is in three parts. Once the lobsters are on the grill, there is time to make the two sauces that give this unusual and delectable dish its characteristic quality. To serve two or four:

Two 1½-pound live lobsters
Olive oil, salt, pepper

½ cup LOBSTER BISQUE BASE (p. 151)*
½ teaspoon minced fresh tarragon
¾ cup cream
1 teaspoon brandy
6 tablespoons butter
1 tablespoon minced parsley
Juice of ¼ lemon
Salt and pepper

PLUNGE the lobsters into a kettle of boiling salted water for 2 minutes, remove them, and let them drain. Place the lobsters on their backs on a wooden board, and split them each in two with a sharp heavy knife, running it from the top of the bodies down through the tails; cut through the shells so that the halves will lie flat. Remove the black veins in the tails, and carefully take out the dark liver (tomalley) and any coral there may be and reserve them.

Season the lobster meat with salt and pepper and brush it all well with olive oil. Grill or broil the lobsters (over charcoal, if possible) for 25 to 30 minutes.

Meanwhile, combine the tomalley and coral, the tarragon, LOBSTER BISQUE BASE, or a substitute, and the cream in a small heavy saucepan. Cook the sauce over high heat, stirring often, until it thickens. Then add the brandy, and keep the sauce warm.

Cream the butter for the second "sauce," or *maître-d'hôtel* butter, and work into it the chopped parsley, a pinch each of salt and freshly ground pepper, and the lemon juice. Mix well and keep in a cool place.

When the lobsters are done, separate the claws from the bodies and crack the claws open. Cut off and split the joints with scissors, and extract the meat; add these small pieces to

---

* Frozen or tinned lobster soup, undiluted, can substitute, if necessary, for lobster bisque base.

the hot sauce. Place the lobsters on a hot platter with their claws, and garnish with sprigs of parsley.

In our restaurant, the waiter will extract the lobster meat at the table and serve it to each diner. A tablespoon of parsley butter will be placed on the meat and the warm sauce will be spooned over that. At home, each person will extract his own meat and be served the two sauces from separate bowls. It is the combination of the cold and warm sauces that makes this a particularly delicious dish.

# Le Soufflé Ike
## *Lobster Soufflé*

Dedicated to General Eisenhower, Supreme Commander of the Allied Powers in Europe and distinguished President of the United States

To SERVE two:

The meat of 1 lobster tail, cooked
2 tablespoons butter
2 tablespoons flour
Pinch of salt
1¼ cups milk
½ cup LOBSTER BISQUE BASE (p. 151)*
Small pinch cayenne
2 egg yolks
½ cup grated Gruyère cheese
6 egg whites

* Frozen or tinned lobster soup, undiluted, can substitute, if necessary, for lobster bisque base.

DICE the cooked lobster tail. Melt the butter in a heavy saucepan and stir in the flour and a pinch of salt, and continue stirring for 2 to 3 minutes. Do not let the mixture brown. Add the milk and stir until the sauce boils. Add the LOBSTER BISQUE BASE, or substitute, a small pinch of cayenne, the egg yolks, and the cheese, and remove immediately from the fire. Stir vigorously until the mixture is well blended, then add the lobster meat and set aside.

In a large bowl, beat the egg whites, starting slowly and gradually beating faster until they are stiff and glossy. Fold the whites gently into the lobster mixture. Butter a medium-size soufflé dish and pour the soufflé batter into it (the dish should be about two-thirds full). Bake the soufflé for 20 to 25 minutes in a moderate (350° F.) oven. Serve immediately.

# V

## Les Poulets
*Chicken*

## Le Caneton
*Duckling*

## Le Gibier
*Small Game*

## *How to Preroast Chicken*

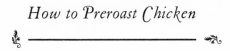

MOST OF the chicken served in our restaurant is preroasted and the cooking is later finished in the sauce that will accompany it. In order that the chicken will not be overcooked, we reduce the usual roasting time by about 10 minutes. Needless to say, the reader who would like a succulent plain roast chicken has only to add 10 to 20 minutes (depending on the size of the bird) to the cooking times in the instructions that follow.

Some of our recipes do require that the bird be fully roasted before the sauce is added, and we indicate this at the outset.

### *To oven-roast a chicken:*

TO SERVE one or two, choose a 1½- to 2-pound chicken that has been well drawn and properly cleaned. Rub it generously inside and out with butter. Lay the bird on its side in an open roasting pan not much larger than the bird itself. Roast it for 40 to 45 minutes at 40 to 45 minutes at 400° F., turning it every 10 minutes.

### *To pot-roast a chicken:*

POT-ROASTING a chicken is done on the top of the stove and presupposes a pot, or *cocotte,* especially designed for the purpose. This utensil is very common in Europe and by now is familiar in your country also. It must be heavy, with high sides, and just large enough to accommodate the chicken.*

---

\* Just such a utensil is, in fact, imported from Belgium, among other countries. Usually oval, it is made of heavy enameled cast iron. ED.

Too large a pot requires more butter than is good for the proper cooking of the bird.

Rub the chicken inside and out with butter as for oven roasting. Brown it in the pot on all sides over moderately high heat for 5 minutes. Turn the bird once more, cover the pot, and reduce the heat to moderate. Continue to cook the chicken for 45 to 50 minutes, turning it every 15 minutes.

*To carve a small chicken:*

CUT OFF together the second joints and drumsticks on either side. Slice the breasts, or cut them from the bone each in one piece, depending on their size; they should not be sliced too thin.

# Le Poulet Grillé du Berger
## *Grilled Chicken with Green Herb Sauce*

Dedicated to Sir Robert Baden-Powell, World Leader of Scouts, who was an inspiration to young and old

THIS delicious way of cooking chicken will be welcomed by those who like to cook over an open fire. Designed for two servings, the recipe can easily be doubled or quadrupled. The sauce is made while the chicken is cooking. ED.

One 2-pound chicken
Salt and pepper
5 tablespoons butter, in all

Prepared mustard
Bread crumbs
1 shallot, minced
1 teaspoon chopped cooked sorrel, *or* canned sorrel
    purée
1 teaspoon chopped parsley
¾ cup dry white wine
2 tablespoons consommé, *or* diluted beef extract
1 teaspoon chopped fresh mint
Several leaves of water cress
2 teaspoons MEAT JELLY (p. 145), *or* substitute

HAVE THE chicken split down the back, leaving the breast intact; bend the two sides back to make the bird lie flat, and salt and pepper it lightly. In a large skillet, heat about two thirds of the butter, and brown the chicken in it when it is sizzling hot, turning to brown both sides. Then remove the chicken from the pan, brush both sides lightly with mustard, and dip in bread crumbs. Place the chicken on a grill over an open charcoal fire (or, lacking this, broil under high heat). Turn it once to cook both sides; it should be done in 15 to 20 minutes.

Meanwhile, in a small heavy saucepan, over moderate heat, cook the shallot, sorrel, and parsley in the remaining butter until the mixture is soft and well blended. In another small saucepan, combine the white wine, the consommé or diluted beef extract, and the mint. Bring to a boil, add the water cress leaves, boil a few seconds longer, and remove from the heat. Force this mixture through a sieve into the butter and shallot mixture, and add the MEAT JELLY, or substitute. Reheat this sauce, stirring with a whisk to blend it well, and season lightly with salt and pepper.

Place the grilled chicken on a hot platter, carve it at the table, and serve the sauce from a sauceboat.

# Le Poulet Marius
*Chicken with White Wine, Tomatoes, and Olives*

TO SERVE TWO:

One 2-pound chicken
Butter
4 small tomatoes
Salt and pepper
2 shallots, minced
⅜ cup dry white wine
¼ clove of garlic, minced
Pinch of saffron
8 small olives
Thinly sliced white bread

FULLY ROAST and carve the chicken according to the directions on page 71. Keep it warm. Pour the butter in which the chicken has cooked into a small skillet, and in it fry the bread, first cut into small lozenges.

While the chicken is roasting, peel, seed, and chop the tomatoes. Simmer them over moderate heat, with a lump of butter and salt and pepper, until they are soft.

In another pan, cook the minced shallots in 2 teaspoons of butter until they are soft, but do not let them brown. Add the white wine, garlic, saffron, olives, and the cooked tomatoes, and simmer all together.

Arrange the chicken on a hot platter, pour the sauce around it, and garnish with the fried croutons and sprigs of water cress.

# Le Poulet de l'Oncle Jules
*Chicken with Green Celery and Butter*

Dedicated to Jules van Zeebroeck, the eminent educator, who understands the true meaning of friendship

 ——————————————

TO SERVE TWO:

One 2-pound chicken
Butter
Young green celery
Dry white wine
Salt and pepper
New potatoes
Minced parsley

PREROAST and carve the chicken according to the directions on page 71.

Meanwhile, cut small very green celery stalks into about a dozen 3-inch lengths. Boil them in lightly salted water for 15 minutes, and drain. Peel and boil 6 or 8 small new potatoes.

Place the chicken in a casserole from which it can be served. Add a generous lump of fresh butter and the celery, season with salt and pepper, and simmer over low heat for 15 minutes. Then add several spoonfuls of dry white wine, and simmer again for a few minutes. The butter sauce will have a delicious flavor and a characteristic light-green color. Baste the pan juices over the chicken, surround it with the potatoes, sprinkle these with chopped parsley, and serve. This dish may, of course, also be presented on a hot platter.

## Le Poulet Mariette
### Chicken in Cream with Pickled Gherkins

To our Cousin Mariette, who has always received us
in her charming home with affection and understanding

TO SERVE two:

One 2-pound chicken
Butter
1¼ cups heavy cream
2 tablespoons tomato purée *
4 teaspoons MEAT JELLY (p. 145), *or* substitute
Salt and pepper
2–3 sour pickled gherkins, finely sliced
Thinly sliced white bread

PREROAST and carve the chicken according to the directions on
page 71. Pour the butter in which the chicken has cooked into
a small skillet, and in it fry the bread, first cut into small
lozenges or squares.

Return the carved chicken to its pan, and place it over the
fire. Add the cream, the tomato purée, and the MEAT JELLY,
or a substitute, and season lightly with salt and pepper. Stir
the sauce and simmer until it is somewhat reduced, then add
the sliced gherkins.

Arrange the chicken on a hot platter, pour the sauce over
it, and garnish with the fried croutons.

* See p. 6 concerning tomato purée.

# Le Poulet d'Astra
*Chicken with Rosé Wine and Fennel Sauce*

TO SERVE two:

One 2-pound chicken
Butter
8 mushroom caps, cooked (p. 153)
1 teaspoon dried fennel
½ cup CHICKEN CONSOMMÉ (p. 145), *or* canned
   chicken broth
⅜ cup rosé wine, preferably rosé d'Anjou
4 teaspoons MEAT JELLY (p. 145), *or* substitute
Salt and pepper


FULLY ROAST and carve the chicken according to the directions on page 71. Prepare the mushrooms according to the basic recipe. Keep both chicken and mushrooms warm if they must wait for the sauce.

Simmer together the fennel and the consommé for several minutes, then strain out the fennel through a fine sieve. Combine this seasoned broth, the wine, and the MEAT JELLY, or a substitute, and add a little salt and pepper. Simmer the sauce until it thickens slightly.

Arrange the chicken on a hot platter, garnish it with the mushrooms, and pour the sauce over all.

# Le Poulet à la Noix de Coco
## *Chicken with Coconut*

TO SERVE two:

One 2-pound chicken
Butter
3 tablespoons whisky
2 tablespoons tomato purée *
4 teaspoons MEAT JELLY (p. 145), *or* substitute
3 tablespoons unsalted butter
1 tablespoon grated coconut
Salt and pepper
Thinly sliced white bread

PREROAST and carve the chicken according to the directions on page 71. Pour the butter in which the chicken has cooked into a small skillet.

Return the carved chicken to the pan in which it was cooked. Add the whisky, touch it with a lighted match, and shake the pan until the flames die out. Add the tomato purée, the MEAT JELLY, or a substitute, and the butter and grated coconut. Season lightly with salt and pepper. Stir well to blend the sauce and remove from the heat as soon as it is hot. Meanwhile, fry the bread, cut into small triangles or lozenges, in the chicken butter.

Arrange the pieces of chicken on a hot platter, pour the sauce over them, and garnish with the fried croutons and sprigs of parsley.

* See p. 6 concerning tomato purée.

# Le Poulet Chantraine Junior
*Chicken in Cream*

To serve two:

One 2-pound chicken
Butter
3 tablespoons gin, *or* brandy
Salt and pepper
1¼ cups heavy cream
4 teaspoons MEAT JELLY (p. 145), *or* substitute
1 teaspoon currant jelly
Thinly sliced white bread

PREROAST and carve the chicken according to the directions on page 71. Pour the butter in which the chicken has cooked into a small skillet.

Return the carved chicken to the pan in which it was cooked. Add the gin, touch it with a lighted match, and shake the pan until the flames die out. Add a little salt and pepper, and add the cream, MEAT JELLY, or a substitute, and currant jelly. Stir well, return the pan to the heat, and cook gently until the sauce thickens. Meanwhile, fry the bread, cut into small triangles or lozenges, in the chicken butter.

Arrange the pieces of chicken on a hot platter, cover with the sauce, garnish with the fried croutons, and serve very hot.

# Le Poulet Nola
## *Chicken with Plus-que-Parfait Sauce*

We dedicate one of our finest recipes to all the heroes
of the last War, especially to those who fought with un-
equal arms, in humble recognition of their great sacrifice
for us

 ————————————

THIS RECIPE demands special attention and must be
made with care. The savory result, however, will
justify the extra work. If you do not have the PÂTÉ
PLUS-QUE-PARFAIT on hand, substitute the finest
liver pâté available in the market. And be sure,
if you must use a substitute for MEAT JELLY,
to choose one also of the finest quality and to salt
the sauce sparingly. To serve two:

One 2-pound chicken
Butter for roasting
2 chicken livers
1 tablespoon Port, Madeira, *or* vermouth
3 tablespoons PÂTÉ PLUS-QUE-PARFAIT (p. 15)
3 tablespoons butter
Salt and pepper
3/8 cup brandy *or* Armagnac
3/4 cup cream
4 teaspoons MEAT JELLY (p. 145), *or* substitute
Thinly sliced white bread

PREROAST and carve the chicken according to the directions on
page 71. Pour the butter in which the chicken has cooked into
a small skillet, and in it fry the bread, first cut into small
lozenges. By the time you are ready to carve the chicken, have
ready all the elements of the following sauce:

Carefully remove any gall from the chicken livers, and in a small bowl marinate them in the Port, Madeira, or vermouth for 1 hour. Then force them through a strainer. Now add to them the pâté and the butter, and with a fork blend all together to form a smooth thick paste.

Return the carved chicken to the pan in which it was cooked and place it over high heat. Add the brandy, touch it with a lighted match, and shake the pan until the flames die out. Now stir in the cream and then the MEAT JELLY, and let the sauce blend and reduce for a few minutes. Then add the pâté-and-liver mixture, stir it well into the liquid in the pan, and simmer gently until the sauce is hot and thickened.

Arrange the carved chicken on a hot platter. Strain the sauce through a fine sieve over the chicken, and garnish with the fried croutons. Serve very hot.

# Le Caneton Alphonsine
### *Roast Duckling with Grapefruit and Cherries*

In memory of the happy days of my childhood

TO SERVE two or three:

1 very young duckling, preferably not over 4 pounds
Butter, salt, and pepper for roasting
2 grapefruit, preferably pink
⅜ cup dry white wine
4 teaspoons granulated sugar
Powdered sugar
¾ cup Port

¼ cup CHERRIES IN SYRUP (p. 158)
5 teaspoons cherry syrup
2½ tablespoons MEAT JELLY (p. 145), *or* substitute
Salt
Paprika

CLEAN THE duck, salt and pepper the inside, and truss the bird. Roast or pot-roast it in butter as you would a chicken (see page 71). Roast it according to the size, 25 to 30 minutes for a very small bird, or up to 50 minutes for a 4- or 5-pound one. By the time the duck is done, have ready all the elements of the sauce that follows.

Pare off thinly the yellow peel or "zest" of one grapefruit, taking care not to include any of the white rind underneath, and mince it finely. In a small saucepan, combine the white wine, grapefruit peel, and 4 teaspoons of sugar, and heat over a moderate fire until the sugar dissolves.

Squeeze all the juice from one grapefruit, strain it, and reserve. Peel the second grapefruit completely, divide it into sections, remove the seeds, and carefully remove all white filaments. Arrange the sections in a small baking dish, sprinkle them with confectioners' sugar, and glaze them in a very hot oven; keep them warm.

In a small covered saucepan, heat the cherries in a few spoonfuls of the Port.

When the duck is done, transfer it to a heatproof dish and place it over low heat. Pour all the fat out of the roasting pan and discard it. Pour the remaining Port into the roasting pan, place it over direct heat, and stir in the white-wine and grapefruit-peel mixture, the reserved grapefruit juice, the Port in which the cherries were warmed, the cherry syrup, and the MEAT JELLY, or substitute. Season lightly with salt and a pinch of paprika, and simmer the sauce until it is reduced and begins to thicken. At the very last, add the cherries.

Carve the duck over the heat on which its dish is standing,

then transfer the pieces to a hot serving platter. Surround with the glazed grapefruit sections, pour the sauce over the duck, and garnish with watercress.

# Le Gibier à la Sauce Bernardine
## *Game Birds with Cream and*
## *Plus-que-Parfait Sauce*

To the fond and vivid memory of my old companions, the Scouts of the CM Group

 ———————————————

THIS SAUCE, one of our most famous, is designed to be served with woodcock or snipe, but it lends itself just as well to other game such as partridge, quail, wild duck, pheasant, hare, etc. The hearts and livers of the game are an essential part of the sauce, and a little of the blood is also used when possible. The proportions given for the sauce in this recipe are for two small game birds to serve two people, but they are easily doubled or tripled. A fine liver pâté may be substituted for the PLUS-QUE-PARFAIT.

2 small game birds
Butter for roasting
2 tablespoons butter
3 tablespoons PÂTÉ PLUS-QUE-PARFAIT (p. 15)
Salt and pepper
⅜ cup brandy or Armagnac
¾ cup cream
4 teaspoons MEAT JELLY (p. 145), *or* substitute
Thinly sliced white bread

DRAW and clean the game birds, reserving the hearts and livers, and preroast them in butter as you would a chicken (see page 71). The roasting time depends, of course, on the size of the birds (15 to 20 minutes for small ones), but be sure to leave them underdone, as they will be cooked again in the sauce. When you remove them from the roasting pan for carving, pour off all the butter. (You may now use this, or fresh butter, to fry the bread, first cut into small strips or triangles, in a separate skillet.) By the time you are ready to carve the birds, have ready all the elements of the sauce that follows.

Force the raw hearts and livers through a sieve. (Or you can purée them in an electric blender. ED.) Be sure first to remove any trace of gall from the livers. In a ceramic bowl, combine the heart-and-liver purée, the softened butter, the pâté, a dash of brandy or Armagnac, and a little blood of the game if possible. Season with salt and pepper, and with a fork blend the mixture to a smooth paste.

Carve the birds, return them to the roasting pan, and place over high heat. Pour the brandy or Armagnac over them, touch it with a lighted match, and shake the pan until the flames die out. Then stir in the cream and the MEAT JELLY, or substitute, and simmer gently, stirring occasionally, until the sauce begins to thicken. Now, off the heat, stir in the liver-and-pâté mixture; return the pan to low heat for a few minutes, until the sauce is hot and well blended.

Place the carved birds on a hot platter and strain the sauce over them, forcing it through the strainer with a heavy spoon. Garnish with the fried croutons and with sprigs of parsley.

# Le Gibier à la Sauce d'Oncle André
*Game Birds with Wine and*
*Plus-que-Parfait Sauce*

To my brother-in-law, who has always extended to me
the affection of a true brother

As with the sauce Bernardine in the previous
recipe, this sauce lends distinction to many kinds of
game. The proportions given here are for enough
sauce to serve three or four. The size and number
of birds should be chosen accordingly.

Game birds
Butter for roasting
3 tablespoons butter
3 tablespoons PÂTÉ PLUS-QUE-PARFAIT (p. 15)
Salt and pepper
1 bunch Muscatel grapes
1 cup sweet white wine
¾ cup Port
¾ cup cream
4 teaspoons MEAT JELLY (p. 145), *or* substitute
Thinly sliced white bread

DRAW AND clean the game birds, reserving the hearts and
livers, and roast them in butter as explained at the beginning of
the recipe for game with SAUCE BERNARDINE. By the time
you are ready to carve the birds and fry the croutons, have
ready all the elements of the sauce.

Prepare the hearts and livers as in the previous recipe, and
combine them with the softened butter, the pâté, a dash of
Port, and a little blood of the game if possible. Season with

85

salt and pepper, and with a fork blend the mixture to a smooth paste.

Peel a dozen of the grapes, and in a small saucepan warm them in a little of the white wine. Crush the remainder of the grapes in a sieve to obtain the juice, and reserve it.

Carve the birds, return them to the roasting pan from which you have poured off all the butter, and place it over high heat. Pour a little more of the white wine and the Port over the birds, and touch with a lighted match. When the flames die out, stir in the rest of the white wine, the cream, and the MEAT JELLY, or a substitute, and simmer gently, stirring occasionally, until the sauce begins to thicken. Now, off the heat, stir in the liver-and-pâté mixture; return the pan to low heat to reduce the sauce again, then stir in the grape juice and blend well.

Place the carved birds on a hot platter and strain the sauce over them, forcing it through a strainer with a heavy spoon. Garnish with the peeled grapes and the fried croutons.

## VI

Les Foies de Volailles
*Chicken Livers*

Les Rognons
*Kidneys*

Les Ris de Veau
*Sweetbreads*

Les Viandes & le Gibier
*Meat & Large Game*

# Les Fonds d'Artichauts Fabiola
## *Artichoke Bottoms with Chicken Livers, Mushrooms, and Truffles*

To Fabiola, Queen of the Belgians, who has conquered the hearts of all her people, we dedicate this most carefully perfected of our recipes in token of our respect and devotion

To SERVE four:

8 large freshly cooked artichoke bottoms (p. 154), *or* canned artichoke bottoms
Butter
½ pound chicken livers
¾ pound mushrooms, cooked (p. 153)
Salt and pepper
2½ tablespoons MEAT JELLY (p. 145), in all, *or* substitute
3 tablespoons Port or Madeira
3 tablespoons diced truffles

TRIM THE livers of any gall or filaments. Prepare the mushrooms and artichokes according to the basic recipes.

Heat 2½ tablespoons of butter in a heavy saucepan. Add the cooked mushrooms and the livers, sprinkle them with salt and pepper, and brown them over a fairly high heat. Remove from the pan with a slotted spoon, and chop finely. Then return the livers and mushrooms to the saucepan, and add half the MEAT JELLY, or substitute. Simmer over a very low heat.

Heat the Port or Madeira, truffles, and the rest of the MEAT JELLY in another saucepan over low heat. Heat the artichoke bottoms in a little butter.

Place the artichokes on a heated serving platter, fill them with the liver-mushroom mixture, and pour the truffle sauce over all.

# Les Fonds d'Artichauts Ninette
### *Artichoke Bottoms with Forcemeat, Chicken Livers, and Truffles*

To our god-daughter

TO SERVE two:

4 freshly cooked artichoke bottoms (p. 154), *or* canned artichoke bottoms
½ pound finely ground mixed pork and veal
1 small onion, minced
1 egg
Salt and pepper
CLEAR MEAT CONSOMMÉ (p. 141), *or* substitute
1 shallot, minced
3 tablespoons Madeira *or* Port
4 tablespoons MEAT JELLY (p. 145), *or* substitute
2 tablespoons diced truffle
2 chicken livers
Butter

PREPARE the artichoke bottoms according to the basic recipe.

Mix the meats, onion, and lightly beaten egg thoroughly, and season with salt and freshly ground black pepper. Shape this forcemeat into tiny balls and poach them in enough simmering consommé almost to cover them for about 10 minutes.

In another saucepan, simmer together the shallot and Madeira or Port for a few minutes. Add the MEAT JELLY, or substitute, and the truffles. Stir and keep warm. Heat 2 teaspoons of butter in a small skillet, and in it brown the chicken livers quickly over high heat; sprinkle with salt and pepper. Reduce the heat and cook the livers just until they are done.

Reheat the artichoke bottoms in another pan with a little butter. Remove the truffles from their pan with a slotted spoon, sprinkle them on the artichoke bottoms, and transfer the artichokes to a heated platter. Surround them with the meat balls and livers, and pour the wine sauce over all.

# Le Rognon "X"
## *Veal Kidneys in Red Wine and Cream*

To our Cousine Lucienne from a grateful uncle

TO SERVE two or four:

2 veal kidneys
Salt and pepper
2 tablespoons butter, for cooking kidneys
2 shallots, minced
2 teaspoons butter, for cooking shallots
¾ cup red wine
⅜ cup heavy cream
2½ tablespoons MEAT JELLY (p. 145), *or* substitute
3 tablespoons tomato purée *
Pinch of sugar
Salt and pepper
2 teaspoons chopped fresh tarragon
Thinly sliced white bread, optional

* See p. 6 concerning tomato purée.

BUY THE veal kidneys with a coating of fat left on them. Split each kidney in two, and sprinkle them with salt and pepper. In a heavy saucepan or skillet, over moderate heat, cook them in the butter for 15 minutes, stirring occasionally. Remove the kidneys from the pan, and cut away the fat. Then cut them into fairly thick slices so that they will not become tough when they are cooked again in the sauce.

While you are making the sauce that follows, you may if you wish, fry the bread, cut into strips or triangles, in the butter in which the kidneys have just been cooked.

In another saucepan, over low heat, cook the minced shallots in butter until they are soft, but do not let them brown. Then turn up the heat, and add the sliced kidneys. Immediately stir in the red wine, cream, MEAT JELLY, or substitute, and the tomato purée, and season with a pinch of sugar and a little salt and pepper. Simmer until the sauce becomes moderately thick, and at the last stir in the chopped tarragon. Serve immediately, garnished with the fried croutons.

## Le Rognon René
### *Flambèed Veal Kidneys with Mustard*

 ——————————————

TO SERVE two or four:

2 veal kidneys
Salt and pepper
6 tablespoons butter, in all
Thinly sliced white bread
½ cup brandy
4 teaspoons MEAT JELLY (p. 145), *or* substitute
2 teaspoons prepared mustard
Minced parsley

BUY THE veal kidneys with a coating of fat left on them, and prepare them as described at the beginning of the previous recipe for Kidneys in Red Wine and Cream. For this preliminary cooking, use half the amount of butter indicated above. Then, when you remove the kidneys from their pan to slice them, pour off all the hot butter into another smaller frying pan; use this to fry the bread, cut into small strips or triangles. This may be done immediately, as the remainder of the cooking is quickly finished.

Return the sliced kidneys to the pan in which they were cooked. Place it over high heat and, as soon as it is hot, add the brandy. Touch it with a lighted match, and shake the pan until the flames die out. Then add the MEAT JELLY, or substitute, and the mustard. Stir well and, when the mixture is heated through, add the remaining butter. Stir until the pan juices and butter are well blended, and serve immediately, garnished with the fried croutons and sprinkled with minced parsley.

## *How to Prepare Sweetbreads*

SWEETBREADS demand very careful attention in their preparation. They may be served in many delicious ways but the precooking is always the same. One pair of veal sweetbreads will serve two people. The following directions are for 1 or 2 pairs.

1 or 2 pairs veal sweetbreads
1 tablespoon diced salt pork or fresh pork fat
1 large onion, sliced
1 large carrot, sliced

1 bay leaf
1 sprig of thyme
2 sprigs of parsley
CLEAR MEAT CONSOMMÉ (p. 141), *or* substitute
Salt and pepper

SOAK THE sweetbreads in lightly salted water for 3 hours. Keep the water cold by putting the bowl in the refrigerator or adding ice cubes.

Remove any traces of bloody tissues and the outer membrane. Transfer the sweetbreads to a saucepan, cover them with lightly salted cold water, and bring slowly to a boil, stirring occasionally with a wooden spoon. As soon as the boiling point is reached, transfer the sweetbreads to a bowl of cold water and place under a faucet of cold running water; keep the water running until the sweetbreads are cool. Then drain them, remove the connecting tissues and nerve filaments, and place the sweetbreads at one end of a dish towel on a flat surface. Cover with the other end of the towel, place a wooden board on top, and weight the board with some heavy object in order to flatten the sweetbreads.

Butter a shallow flameproof baking dish, and put in it the diced pork fat, the sliced vegetables, and the herbs tied into a bouquet. Arrange the sweetbreads on top of these ingredients, and add enough CLEAR MEAT CONSOMMÉ (a good substitute or even cold water will do) to cover. Sprinkle lightly with salt and pepper. Cover the pan, and cook the sweetbreads over low heat or in a 300° F. oven for 30 to 40 minutes. Sweetbreads must never be exposed to high heat or they will disintegrate. Baste them with the cooking liquid as it reduces.

Unless the sweetbreads are to be prepared to serve immediately, transfer them to a china or ceramic bowl, and strain the cooking liquid over them. Cool them completely before storing in the refrigerator. The liquid is drained off before the sweetbreads are finally prepared for serving with a sauce.

# Le Ris de Veau Pierre-Ange
## *Sweetbreads with Tomato Sauce*

To our dear cousin and delightful companion, Pierre Angelroth

 ————————————

TO SERVE four:

2 pairs veal sweetbreads
Lightly beaten egg white, flour, and butter for cooking sweetbreads
2 carrots
¼ pound butter, in all, for sauces
4 teaspoons flour
⅜ cup tomato purée *
1¼ cups CLEAR MEAT CONSOMMÉ (p. 141), *or* substitute
2 teaspoons sugar
Heavy cream, optional
Salt and pepper
1 tablespoon chopped parsley
Juice of ¼ lemon
Thinly sliced white bread, optional

\* See p. 6 concerning tomato purée.

PRECOOK the sweetbreads according to the directions on page 93.

Scrape the carrots and slice them thinly. In a heavy saucepan, over moderate heat, simmer them with a quarter of the butter and a pinch each of salt and sugar for about 10 minutes. Then stir in the flour and, when it is well blended in, add the tomato purée. Simmer again for another 10 minutes, then add the CLEAR MEAT CONSOMMÉ, or substitute, and the sugar. (If you use a commercial beef consomme, it may already be sweetened and the sugar should then be omitted. ED.) Let the sauce reduce over low heat for 45 minutes. Then strain it, and correct the seasoning. A little cream may be added if you wish. In this case, bring the sauce to a boil again, add the cream, and again check the seasoning. Keep the sauce warm.

Make the second "sauce," or *maître-d'hôtel* butter, by creaming the remaining butter and working into it the chopped parsley, a pinch each of salt and freshly ground pepper, and the lemon juice. Mix well and keep in a cool place.

Dip the sweetbreads first in the beaten egg white and then lightly in flour. In a skillet, over low heat, melt a generous lump of butter, and cook the sweetbreads in it, covered, turning them once, until they are well heated through. Arrange them on a hot platter. If you wish, the bread, first cut into strips of triangles, may now be fried in the butter remaining in the skillet and used to garnish the platter.

The tomato sauce and the *maître-d'hôtel* butter are served from separate sauceboats or bowls. Place a portion of the butter on each helping, then cover with tomato sauce.

# Le Ris de Veau Michèle
## *Sweetbreads in White Wine*

THIS DISH is made up of several component parts. Read the whole recipe before starting to make it. To serve two:

1 pair veal sweetbreads
½ recipe MUSHROOM DUXELLES (p. 154)
2 tomatoes
4 cooked artichoke bottoms (p. 154), *or* canned artichoke bottoms

Butter, salt, pepper
¾ cup dry white wine
2 tablespoons tomato purée *
Thinly sliced white bread, optional

PRECOOK the sweetbreads according to the directions on page 93.

Prepare half the recipe for MUSHROOM DUXELLES, and keep it warm.

Peel, halve, and carefully seed the tomatoes. Cut them in pieces and simmer them gently with butter and salt and pepper until they are heated through.

Prepare the artichoke bottoms according to the basic recipe. Warm them in a little butter, and fill them with the *duxelles* when you are ready to serve the sweetbreads.

In a skillet, over low heat, melt a generous lump of butter and cook the sweetbreads in it, turning them once, just until they are well heated through. Then pour off all the butter in the skillet. The butter may now be used to fry the bread, first cut into strips or triangles, if you wish to garnish the platter with croutons. Stir the white wine and tomato purée into the skillet, and simmer gently until the sauce reduces a little.

Arrange the sweetbreads on a hot platter, pour the sauce over them, and surround with the filled artichoke bottoms, the tomatoes, and the croutons.

This dish is also sometimes garnished with a few small meat balls cooked in consommé. Directions for making these are in the recipe for FONDS D'ARTICHAUTS NINETTE on page 90.

* See p. 6 concerning tomato purée.

WE GIVE you very few recipes for meat or large game. This is because the classic methods for roasting and grilling meat cannot be improved upon and are described in many cookbooks. Also, a wide variety of meats is served at our restaurant with either SAUCE CHANTRAINE or SAUCE SECRET DE TANTE FÉLICIE, two of our favorite original creations for which the recipes are given on pages 39 and 42. Four more of our meat or game specialties follow.

# La Piece de Boeuf Marie-Agnès
## *Roast Sirloin of Beef*

TO SERVE three or four:

2-pound piece boneless sirloin of beef *
½-pound piece flank of beef
Salt and pepper
Butter

HAVE THE boneless sirloin well trimmed and tied for roasting. Season both the roast and the piece of flank of beef well with salt and pepper. In a large skillet, heat a generous lump of butter until it begins to smoke. Brown both pieces of meat in it on all sides.

* The small piece of beef intended here is what is called on the Continent the *contre-filet*. In this country it is called eye of sirloin. To obtain exactly this cut, you may have to order it especially. However, the delicious method of roasting described in this recipe can, of course, be applied to any fine boneless cut of beef that can be roasted, including the fillet or tenderloin. ED.

Transfer the sirloin to a small roasting pan. Cut the piece of flank into chunks, and add them and a lump of fresh butter to the roasting pan. (The purpose of the flank meat is solely to contribute a rich pan juice.) Roast the meat in a pre-heated 400° F. oven for 12 to 15 minutes per pound. Serve the sirloin sliced, on a hot platter, surrounded with small boiled potatoes, and with the pan juice strained over it.

# Le Plat des Distingués
## *Gratinéed Veal*

VEAL cooked in this manner is one of our restaurant's most popular dishes. Other meats (such as boned chicken breasts or pork) may also be prepared in the same way. The proportions in this recipe are to serve two, but the dish is not a difficult one and the ingredients may easily be doubled or tripled. To serve two:

4 veal scallops (about ¾ pound) *
2 tablespoons butter, or more if needed
4–5 mushrooms, cooked (p. 153)
⅜ cup heavy cream
3 tablespoons grated Swiss cheese
¾ cup dry white wine
4 teaspoons MEAT JELLY (p. 145), *or* substitute

---

* Various cuts of veal may be used but one of the best is leg of veal. Ask your butcher to slice the meat about 3/8 of an inch thick, to trim it of all fat and tendons, and to pound the slices evenly to about 1/4 of an inch.

SEASON the veal well with salt and pepper. Heat the butter in a large heavy skillet, and brown the slices in it on each side. Add more butter if necessary to prevent scorching, and allow about 20 minutes cooking time. They should be well browned, tender, and almost completely cooked.

Have ready in advance the remaining ingredients: Prepare the mushrooms according to the basic recipe. Drain and slice them, and, in a small saucepan, combine them with the cream and about one third of the grated cheese. Simmer all together, stirring often, until the mixture thickens. Set aside.

When the veal is done, arrange the slices in a shallow baking dish, mask them with the mushroom mixture, and sprinkle with the remaining cheese. Brown quickly in a hot (450° F.) oven.

Put the skillet in which the veal was cooked over high heat. Stir the white wine into the hot skillet, then add the MEAT JELLY, or substitute, and simmer this sauce, stirring well, until it is reduced and begins to thicken. Pour it over the gratinéed veal and serve immediately.

# Le Râble de Lièvre à la Sauce Jenny
## Saddle of Hare with Sauce Jenny

THIS SAUCE for saddle of hare was created and bequeathed to us by a true friend whose name it bears. Jenny died at the age of eighty-four, after a wonderful life during which her warmth and generosity and her exceptional cooking gladdened many hearts. To serve three or four:

Saddle of young hare *
Butter, salt, pepper
Liver of the hare
2 tablespoons butter
1 bay leaf
1 sprig of thyme
6 shallots, peeled
1 stalk of celery
1 carrot
3 tablespoons red wine, preferably Bordeaux
1 cup heavy cream
Blood of the hare, optional
4 teaspoons currant jelly
3 tablespoons brandy
2 teaspoons granulated sugar
Juice of 1 lemon
Salt and pepper

PLACE THE dressed saddle of hare in a shallow well-buttered roasting pan; remove the thin membrane that covers the back. Butter the surface of the saddle and salt and pepper it lightly. Roast it for 20 to 30 minutes in a pre-heated 400° F. oven. To check that the hare is properly cooked, lift it from the pan; the juice that runs from it should be slightly pink. (If you prefer hare well done, the juice should be colorless, but we do not think this is preferable.) By the time the hare is done, have ready the following sauce, which is cooked separately.

Put the liver of the hare in a saucepan with the butter and herbs, and add the vegetables, washed and cut in pieces, and a spoonful of water. Salt and pepper lightly, and simmer,

* The saddle is the back of the hare, extending from behind the shoulders to the thighs. A domestic rabbit that has been marinated in a game marinade makes a good substitute, but it would be wise to include the back legs since rabbits are smaller and less meaty.

covered, over low heat for about 30 minutes. Remove the liver and force it through a fine sieve (or purée it in an electric blender) into a small saucepan. Add the red wine, blend the mixture well with a whisk, and simmer it over very low heat for 15 minutes. Then add the cream and, if possible, 3 or 4 tablespoons of the blood of the hare. Let this mixture simmer again over low heat until it begins to thicken. Now add the currant jelly, brandy, sugar, and lemon juice, and heat and stir until the sauce is well blended. Season to taste with salt and pepper.

Carve the hare on a hot platter and serve the sauce from a sauceboat.

# Le Festival Culinaire
## *Wild Game with Chestnuts*

This recipe is dedicated to Monsieur Arthur Haulot, General Commissioner of Belgian Tourism, whose love of Belgium is happily communicated to both Belgians and foreigners. His interest in gastronomy, which he considers one of the great attractions of our country, has led him to our restaurant, which he is kind enough to call one of the best.

 ————————————

WE SERVE the sauce in this recipe with venison and also with young wild boar. It is suitable for any other kind of game as well. To serve two:

1–1¼ pounds young boar *or* venison steak
Butter, salt, pepper
1 pound chestnuts in their shells, *or* canned chestnuts
    packed in brine

Milk
Water
1 stalk of celery
Pinch of sugar
2½ tablespoons MEAT JELLY (p. 145), *or* substitute
2 tomatoes
3 tablespoons brandy
1 cup heavy cream
1 teaspoon tomato paste
Thinly sliced white bread, optional

TRIM A piece of young boar or venison steak suitable for pan-frying, and salt and pepper it. In a heavy skillet, heat well a generous lump of butter, and brown the steak in it, on both sides, until it is almost but not quite done; it will be cooked further in the sauce. Remove the steak from the skillet, carve it, and keep it warm. In advance, prepare the ingredients for the sauce so that they will be at hand when the steak is ready.

With a sharp knife, slash a cross in the shells of the chestnuts on the flat side of each nut. Plunge them into boiling water for a few moments, then scoop them out a few at a time with a small strainer, and peel off both the shells and the skins that cover the nuts. If this is done while the nuts are hot, it is not difficult.

Put the chestnuts in a heavy saucepan and add a mixture of 1 part milk and 2 parts water, enough liquid to cover them well. Add the celery and a good pinch of·sugar, and simmer the chestnuts, covered, for 15 to 20 minutes, or until they are tender. Then, with a slotted spoon, remove them to another small heavy saucepan, and add the MEAT JELLY, or substitute. Over moderate heat, let the chestnuts caramelize lightly, and keep them warm.*

* If prepared chestnuts in brine are used, they must be of the best quality. They need only to be heated in the water-and-milk mixture before they are drained and put to glaze in the MEAT JELLY. ED.

Wash the tomatoes, cut them into pieces, and simmer them over moderate heat with a lump of butter and salt and pepper. Cook until they are soft and reduced but do not let them brown. Force the tomatoes through a fine sieve, and set aside.

When the steak is carved, pour off all the butter from the pan in which it was cooked. The butter may now be used to fry the bread, first cut into strips or triangles, if you wish to garnish the platter with croutons.

Return the carved meat to its skillet, and place over high heat. Pour the brandy over the meat, touch it with a lighted match, and shake the pan until the flames die out. Then stir in the cream, the strained tomatoes, and the tomato paste, and salt and pepper lightly. Bring the sauce to a boil, then simmer it gently, stirring occasionally. You may now remove the meat to a hot serving platter and keep it warm, or let it remain a little longer in the sauce if you feel it needs further cooking. In any case, the sauce is ready when it is somewhat reduced and begins to thicken. It may be thinned with a little water and cream if it thickens too rapidly, and seasoned again accordingly.

Pour the sauce over the meat on the platter, and surround with the glazed chestnuts and the croutons.

# VII

## Les Fruits Accommodés aux Sauces Diverses
*Fruit Desserts*

## Les Sabayons
*Zabaglione*

## Soufflé * Mousse

## Glaces & Sorbets
*Ice Cream & Sherbet*

## Les Crêpes
*Dessert Crêpes*

# Le Dessert de Tante Marie
## *Melon with Wild Strawberries*

In memory of our kindly Aunt Marie, who worked so ceaselessly all her life

NOTHING can compare with the flavor of wild strawberries in this dessert but, of course, it is also delicious with fresh currants, raspberries, cherries, or cultivated strawberries.

Small ripe melons
Wild strawberries or other berries
Sugar
Kirsch

CHOOSE small melons of uniform size and shape. Cut off the top quarters, which will later form the lids. Remove all the seeds and filaments. Then scoop out the flesh, being sure not to pierce the rinds. Dice the flesh evenly and, in a china or ceramic bowl, combine it with the berries. Flavor the mixture to taste with sugar and kirsch, and mix gently but thoroughly. Fill the melon shells to the brim with the fruit and juice, cover with the lids, and chill well before serving.

## Les Fraises des Bois de Mon Oncle
### *Wild Strawberries with Whipped Cream*

To SERVE four:

1 quart wild strawberries, *or* small cultivated strawberries
¾ cup heavy cream
2–3 tablespoons granulated sugar
2 tablespoons currant jelly, preferably homemade
1 teaspoon kirsch

RINSE AND hull the berries, drain them well, and chill.

Whip the cream, then beat in gently the sugar, to taste, the
currant jelly, strained, and the kirsch. Chill.

Serve the berries from a glass bowl with the cream poured
over them and accompanied by plain cookies or lady fingers.

## Les Fraises à la Sauce Martine
### *Strawberries with Port and Currant Jelly Sauce*

To our little grand-daughter, Martine, God grant that
her smile stay always as radiant as we have known it

HERE IS a dessert that is simple to make, yet exquisite to eat. We prefer to use wild strawberries
but, of course, small ripe cultivated berries will also

be very good and many other fruits may be prepared in the same way as well. To serve two or
three:

1 pint wild strawberries, *or* small cultivated strawberries
½ cup currant jelly, preferably homemade
2 tablespoons Port
1 teaspoon orange liqueur, such as Cointreau *or*
Triple-Sec

RINSE AND hull the berries, drain them well, and chill.

Combine the remaining ingredients in a china or ceramic
bowl, blend until the jelly dissolves completely and the sauce
is smooth (strain, if necessary), and chill.

Serve the berries from a glass bowl with the sauce poured
over them and accompanied by plain cookies or lady fingers.

# La Pêche Angali
## *Peaches with Raspberry Sauce*

Dedicated to Charlotte Claereboudt-d'Hauwe, a faithful collaborator whose intelligent initiative and constant
devotion have been so helpful

THE NAME of this recipe, meaning "never enough"
in a Hindu dialect, was bestowed by an enthusiastic
guest. The dessert may also be prepared with yellow
peaches, apricots, strawberries, pineapple, etc. To
serve three or four:

4–5 ripe white peaches
1 pint raspberries
½ cup granulated sugar
Juice of ¼ lemon
Juice of ¼ grapefruit
Slivered blanched almonds

CHILL THE peaches in the refrigerator.

Hull the raspberries, and press them through a strainer, collecting the juice in a china or ceramic bowl. Add the sugar, the lemon and grapefruit juices, mix well, and chill in the refrigerator for at least 1 hour.

Peel the peaches, and slice them into a dessert bowl. Cover with the raspberry sauce, sprinkle with the slivered almonds, and serve with plain cookies or lady fingers.

## Le Pamplemousse Denise
### Grapefruit with Tangerines and Orange Liqueur

To Denise, who brings us another radiant smile to illuminate our home

TO SERVE TWO:

2–3 small grapefruit
2 small tangerines
Slivered blanched almonds
Sugar
Orange liqueur, such as Cointreau *or* Triple-Sec

SLICE OFF the stem ends of the grapefruit, about a quarter of the way down, and reserve them to use as lids. With a thin sharp knife, cut perpendicularly all around the edge of the pulp to free it from the skins; be careful not to pierce the grapefruit shells. Then cut out each section, remove the seeds, and remove all the white filaments in the shells. Be sure to catch all the juice, and return it, with the fruit, to the shells. If there is not enough fruit to fill them, add a few pieces from the third grapefruit.

Peel the tangerines, separate the sections, carefully remove all the white filaments and the seeds, and arrange the sections on top of the grapefruit. Sprinkle with sugar and slivered almonds, and add a good dash of orange liqueur. Cover the grapefruit with their lids, and chill them well. We serve these grapefruit in individual bowls of crushed ice.

## Le Dessert de Marcelle
*Bananas and Cream*

To SERVE four:

4 bananas
¾ cup heavy cream
Juice of 2 lemons
6 tablespoons granulated sugar

MASH THOROUGHLY or sieve the bananas. Mix them with the cream, and blend in the lemon juice, strained, and sugar to taste. Chill thoroughly.

Serve very cold in small goblets or parfait glasses, with lady fingers.

## Les Fruits à la Crème Oubliée
### *Cut-up Fruit with Cream and Wine*

Dedicated to Joseph Chantraine, pioneer in aviation

THIS IS another very simple dessert but, nevertheless, it is unusually delicious. It is served with plain cookies or lady fingers. To serve three or four:

Cut-up fruit (peaches, apricots, strawberries, oranges, pineapple, etc.)
¾ cup heavy cream
2 tablespoons Port *or* Madeira
⅜ cup cherry syrup (p. 158)
3 tablespoons granulated sugar, or to taste

MIX the cream, Port, and cherry syrup in a bowl, add the sugar to taste, and chill the sauce in the refrigerator for 1 hour.

Prepare the fruit, using any combination that seems best according to the season. Serve it well-chilled, in a glass bowl, with the sauce poured over it.

## Les Fruits à la Crème Yvette
### *Cut-up Fruit with Cream*

To my beloved wife, Yvette

TO SERVE two or three:

Cut-up fruit (peaches, strawberries, pears, oranges, bananas, pineapple, grapes, etc.)
¾ cup heavy cream

Granulated sugar to taste
Juice of 1 lemon, or to taste

STIR TOGETHER the cream and sugar until the sugar dissolves.
Add the lemon juice, and continue stirring briskly until the
cream begins to thicken. Chill well.

Prepare the fruit, using any combination that seems best
according to the season. Serve it well-chilled, in a glass bowl,
with the cream poured over it and accompanied by plain cookies
or lady fingers.

# Les Fruits à la Sauce Thérèse
## *Cut-up Fruit with Port and Brandy*

In honor of a young saint beloved the world over

TO SERVE four or more:

Cut-up fruit (oranges, grapefruit, strawberries,
    peaches, bananas, pears, greengage plums, etc.)
¾ cup Port *or* Madeira
4–5 tablespoons granulated sugar, or to taste
Juice of 1 lemon
3 tablespoons brandy

IN A china or glass bowl, combine the Port, sugar, and lemon
juice, and stir until the sugar dissolves; the amount of sugar
depends on the sweetness of the wine and fruit. Chill.

Prepare the fruit, using any combination that seems best
according to the season. Serve it well chilled, in a glass bowl,
with the wine poured over it.

# Les Fruits à la Sauce du Contrôleur
## *Fruit in Brandy and Butter Sauce*

THE COMBINATION of fruits suggested here is a good one, but many others may be used providing they are ripe and juicy. The amount of sugar and type of liqueur used may be varied accordingly. To serve two:

1 large ripe pear
1 orange
1 banana
3 tablespoons butter
3 tablespoons granulated sugar
3 tablespoons brandy
⅜ cup white wine
Split blanched almonds

PEEL, core, and quarter the pear. Peel the orange, remove all the white filaments, and slice it thickly or quarter it; remove the seeds. Peel and halve the banana.

In a heavy saucepan, over low heat, mix together the butter and sugar, and stir until the sugar is well dissolved in the butter. Add the fruit, prick the pieces well with a fork to release their juice, and simmer them gently until they are lightly caramelized.

Now turn up the heat, add the brandy, and touch it with a lighted match. Shake the pan until the flames die out, then add the white wine. Cook a little longer, basting the fruit constantly with the pan juices, and add the split almonds. Serve as soon as the sauce becomes syrupy, on heated dessert plates, and accompanied by plain cookies or lady fingers.

# Les Poires à la Sauce Joséphine
## *Pears with Orange Sauce*

To my mother-in-law, Joséphine Saussus, who was a sweet and understanding lady as well as an excellent cook

OTHER fruit, such as pineapple, bananas, eating apples, grapes, and plums, can be prepared in the same manner. To serve two:

3 oranges
Powdered sugar
Butter
2 perfect ripe pears
Slivered blanched almonds
3 tablespoons granulated sugar
3 tablespoons orange liqueur, such as Cointreau *or* Triple-Sec

GRATE finely the peel of two of the oranges, being careful to take only the thin orange part. Peel the oranges, divide them into sections, and remove carefully all the white filaments and seeds. Arrange the sections in one layer in a shallow buttered pan, and sprinkle them with powdered sugar. Cook them over high heat, turning them in a few minutes, until they acquire a brown glaze on each side.

Squeeze and strain the juice of the third orange and reserve it.

Peel the pears and stud them with thin slivers of blanched almonds. Stand them in a small heavy saucepan, add a lump of butter, and sprinkle them with the sugar and orange rind. Heat the pears slowly, then add the orange juice, and continue to cook until the sauce is lightly caramelized; baste the pears with the sauce occasionally.

Then turn up the heat, pour in the orange liqueur, and

touch it with a lighted match. When the flames die out, add the glazed orange sections, and baste them with the sauce.

Serve immediately, on heated dessert plates, with the orange sections surrounding the pears.

## Ma Pomme
*Poached Apples with Vanilla and Raisin Sauce*

To SERVE four or six:

½ recipe VANILLA PASTRY CREAM (p. 160)
4–6 finest cooking apples
2¼ cups granulated sugar
1 quart boiling water
2 tablespoons lemon juice
2 teaspoons vanilla extract
½ cup seedless raisins
2 teaspoons kirsch
Macaroon crumbs

PREPARE the VANILLA PASTRY CREAM.

Choose apples of uniform size. Remove the cores with an apple corer, and peel. In a saucepan, combine the sugar, boiling water, lemon juice, and vanilla. Bring the syrup to a boil, stirring frequently, then add the apples, and poach them until they are tender; do not overcook. Remove the apples carefully with a slotted spoon. (The syrup may be used again for poaching other fruit. ED.)

Stir the raisins and kirsch into the pastry cream. Arrange the apples in a pretty pottery dish, pour the pastry-cream sauce around them, and sprinkle with the macaroon crumbs.

These apples may also be served with sweetened whipped cream.

# Le Sabayon de l'Anniversaire
## *Zabaglione*

 ————————————————

THIS IS a delicious dessert, one of the quickest to prepare and one of the easiest to spoil. Below are the ingredients for two servings. They can be doubled, trebled, or quadrupled although, in these larger quantities, it is well to reduce slightly the amount of liquid.

1½ tablespoons (4½ teaspoons) Port *or* Madeira
1½ tablespoons (4½ teaspoons) dry white wine
2 egg yolks
5 teaspoons fine granulated sugar

PUT ALL the ingredients in a small, very heavy saucepan with high sides. (Or, you may use a double boiler, though this lengthens the cooking time; have rapidly boiling water in the bottom pan. ED.)

Before putting the pan over heat, beat the mixture well with a sauce whisk. The classical method for whipping is to form the number 8 in the pan with the whisk, hitting the four sides of the pan as you beat. The noise this makes should be like the sound of an old-fashioned train leaving the station, starting slowly and gradually getting up speed—that is the secret, to start slowly and work up to a fast pace bit by bit.

When the mixture is frothy, place the pan over moderately high heat, and continue to beat it without stopping. Watch very carefully: If the zabaglione is successful, it will swell and thicken, fine bubbles will form on the top, and a light curl of steam will float up from it. Remove immediately from the heat. All this may take some time and you must not once stop beating, so call for help if necessary.

Pour the zabaglione into porcelain cups or stemmed glasses, and serve immediately.

## Le Sabayon Fielding
### *Zabaglione with Liqueur*

Dedicated to our faithful and sympathetic friend, the dynamic and well-known Temple Fielding

THIS IS a variation of the preceding recipe for SABAYON DE L'ANNIVERSAIRE. It is difficult to make a zabaglione swell if it contains very much alcohol, therefore the liqueur must be added at the last.

Follow the preceding recipe exactly. When it is about ready, still over the heat and without stopping the whipping, add 1 teaspoon of brandy, or of any other good liqueur such as Cointreau, kirsch, etc. Whip rapidly for a few seconds, and serve immediately.

In multiplying the recipe, allow about 1 teaspoon of liqueur for each 2 egg yolks used.

# Le Sabayon Bobby
*Zabaglione with Champagne*

Dedicated to the Reverend Robert van der Hofstadt, scholar and true friend, whose loyalty has been so steadfast

IN THIS zabaglione, Champagne or another fine white wine, such as Vouvray, Pouilly-Fumé, or Muscadet, is substituted for the combined Port and white wine in the recipe for SABAYON DE L'ANNIVERSAIRE. The total quantity of liquid remains the same. To serve two:

3 tablespoons Champagne or other dry white wine
2 egg yolks
5 teaspoons fine granulated sugar
½ teaspoon finely grated grapefruit rind

THE GRAPEFRUIT rind is added to the other ingredients at the beginning. Proceed exactly as described on page 117.

# Le Soufflé Freedman
*Mint and Ginger Soufflé*

TO SERVE two:

1¼ cups milk
3 tablespoons fine granulated sugar
Pinch of salt

Vanilla bean, *or* ½ teaspoon vanilla extract
2 scant tablespoons flour
3 tablespoons mint syrup, *or* 2 tablespoons white
*crème de menthe*
1 teaspoon minced preserved ginger
1 teaspoon brandy
2 egg yolks, lightly beaten
4 egg whites
Butter
Confectioners' sugar

IN A saucepan, combine the milk, sugar, and salt, and add the vanilla bean if you have one. Bring to a boil, then remove the vanilla bean.

In a small bowl, blend to a thin paste the flour and a spoonful of cold milk. Add this to the hot milk, and add the mint syrup or *crème de menthe,* the minced ginger, and the brandy. Bring the mixture back to a boil, and simmer for 3 or 4 minutes, stirring often with a wooden spoon. Now add the vanilla extract if you did not use a vanilla bean.

Remove the saucepan from the heat and, with a whisk, beat in the egg yolks and 2 teaspoons of butter. Let this cool.

Meanwhile, beat the egg whites stiff. It is well known that egg whites can be beaten to a greater volume in an unlined copper bowl; however, whatever equipment you usually use for beating them will be satisfactory. Butter a soufflé dish and sprinkle it lightly with sugar.

Fold the beaten whites gently into the flavored yolk-and-milk mixture. Spoon the batter into the soufflé dish, and smooth the top with a spatula. Bake the soufflé in a preheated 350° F. oven for 15 to 20 minutes. When it is almost done, sprinkle the soufflé with confectioners' or icing sugar, raise the oven temperature to 450° F., and bake another few minutes, until the top is glazed and lightly browned. Serve immediately.

# La Symphonie Achevée
## *Chocolate Mousse with Cherries*

Dedicated to Maurice Ravel, whose genius was equalled
only by his modesty

 ────────────────

To serve six or eight:

10 squares (10 ounces) Dutch or Swiss bittersweet
   chocolate
6 eggs, separated
Cherries in syrup (p. 158)

In the top of a double boiler, over simmering water, melt the
chocolate, first broken in pieces. With a small whisk, blend it
to a smooth paste, then add the egg yolks, one by one, whisking
hard after each addition. Transfer to a large bowl.

Whip the egg whites stiff, and fold them into the chocolate
mixture. Mix together well but gently, mix in a dozen or so
cherries, and pour the mousse into a glass serving bowl or
individual dessert bowls. Let stand at room temperature for
several hours before chilling in the refrigerator.

This dessert may be garnished before serving with sweetened
whipped cream.

## Le Sorbet Astrid aux Fraises
*Strawberry Sherbet*

In loving memory of the queen who won all our hearts

To SERVE eight or ten:

Sugar syrup (p. 162)
3 pints strawberries
4 oranges
1½ lemons
2¼ cups granulated sugar
1½ cups Port
1½ cups semisweet white wine
Dash of kirsch

MAKE THE sugar syrup and let it cool.

Rinse and hull the srawberries, and force them through a strainer or food mill. Grate the orange and lemon rinds, taking care to use only the thin outer peel. Then, with a knife, peel the fruit completely, cut it into pieces, and remove all the white filaments and seeds. Force the fruit and the grated rinds through the strainer or food mill also. In a china or ceramic bowl, combine this fruit juice, the strawberry purée, and the sugar, Port, white wine, and kirsch. Stir well to dissolve the sugar, and let stand for 1 hour.

Combine the fruit mixture and the cooled sugar syrup, and freeze in an ice-cream freezer. Freeze until as firm as possible; sherbet, however, will not become as firm as ice cream.

Serve in chilled goblets, with lady fingers or plain cookies.

# Le Sorbet Astrid aux Framboises
## *Raspberry Sherbet*

TO SERVE four:

1 pint raspberries
½ cup granulated sugar
Juice of ¼ lemon
Juice of ¼ grapefruit
1½ pints VANILLA ICE CREAM, approximately
    (p. 163)
2 teaspoons kirsch

PREFERABLY, make your own VANILLA ICE CREAM.

Force the raspberries through a fine sieve into a china or ceramic bowl. Add the sugar and strained fruit juices, and stir well to dissolve the sugar. Let stand for 1 hour, then chill in the refrigerator.

Let the ice cream soften a little. Combine it with the raspberry syrup, using 2 parts ice cream to 1 part syrup. Add the kirsch, and beat the mixture well; it should have the consistency of a smooth thick mousse. Serve immediately in chilled goblets, with lady fingers or plain cookies.

A similar sherbet may be made with vanilla ice cream and strained currant jelly. This is a good dessert but the flavor, of course, does not compare with that of the original recipe.

# Le Sorbet de Marc
## *Orange and Grapefruit Sherbet*

To SERVE eight or ten:

Sugar syrup (p. 162)
6 oranges, in all
2 grapefruit, in all
1¾ cups granulated sugar
1¼ cups semisweet white wine
⅜ cup red wine, such as Bordeaux *or* Beaujolais
3 tablespoons kirsch

MAKE THE sugar syrup and let it cool.

Grate the rinds of 2 oranges and 1 grapefruit, taking care to use only the thin outer peel. Then, with a knife, peel all the fruit completely, cut it into pieces, and remove all the white filaments and seeds. Force the fruit and grated rinds through a strainer or food mill into a china or ceramic bowl. Add the sugar, white wine, red wine, and kirsch. Stir well to dissolve the sugar, and let stand for 1 hour. Then combine with the cooled sugar syrup, and freeze in an ice-cream freezer until as firm as possible.

Serve in chilled goblets, with lady fingers or plain cookies.

# La Coupe Cyprès
## *Vanilla Ice Cream with Tangerines and Kirsch*

In honor of Monsieur Eric Cyprès, eminent Counsel of Public Relations

THIS IS a simple and very pretty dessert. To serve six:

1 quart VANILLA ICE CREAM (p. 163)
2–3 tangerines
Kirsch
Slivered blanched almonds

FILL A silver or crystal bowl with a smooth mound of VANILLA ICE CREAM, and scoop out a small hole at the top. Keep very cold.

Peel the tangerines, separate the sections, and carefully remove the white filaments and seeds. Arrange the sections in a circle, like the spokes of a wheel, on top of the ice cream, and sprinkle them with the chopped almonds. Pour a little kirsch into the hole in the center, and serve immediately, accompanied by plain cookies.

## Le Dessert de Tintin
### *Cherries with Chocolate Cream and Ice Cream*

To Monsieur Hervé, the well-known creator of "Tintin," beloved by children of all ages and their parents

THIS DESSERT is a combination of three preparations which are best made a day in advance.

CHERRIES IN SYRUP (p. 158)
Kirsch
CHOCOLATE CREAM (p. 161)
VANILLA ICE CREAM (p. 163)


CHILL THE CHOCOLATE CREAM overnight. Store the VANILLA ICE CREAM where it will stay well frozen.

To serve the dessert, use chilled individual glass or porcelain dessert bowls. Put 3 or 4 cherries in each bowl with a little of their syrup, and add a few drops of kirsch. Cover them with about 2 tablespoons of chocolate cream, and put over this a portion of vanilla ice cream. Serve immediately, with plain cookies or lady fingers.

## *How to Prepare Crêpes*

CRÊPES, or thin dessert pancakes, are one of our most popular specialties. They are cooked in full view of our guests, though the crêpe batter is made ahead as it is better if it stands for at least an hour. Uncle René, who presides over the crêpes in our restaurant, always insists on making them just before they are served, disdaining what he calls *crêpes de tiroir,* or crêpes that have been stored away in a drawer, so to speak. However, making them on the spot, of course, may not be possible at home and crêpes made in advance are a great convenience, particularly if you are making a large quantity.

Though the basic crêpes for these desserts are always the same, they are embellished in many different ways. They are cooked in exactly the same way, whether they are to be served immediately or not. Stack them one on top of the other as they are done; never spread them out on the platter until you are ready to serve them or they will dry out. If the final preparation of the crêpes requires that they be blazed, this must be done over heat on a very hot platter or chafing dish so that the brandy or liqueurs will flame satisfactorily.

The amount of batter in this recipe make 14 to 16 crêpes, depending on the size of the pan and how thin you manage to make them. Allow two or three crêpes per person, according to the richness of the sauce or filling.

1 cup less 2 tablespoons sifted flour
2 eggs
1¼ cups cold milk
Pinch of salt
Pinch of sugar
2 tablespoons butter, melted

*The batter:* Put the sifted flour in a deep bowl, and make a well in the center. Break the eggs into it and, with a wooden spoon, gradually work the flour into the eggs. When the mixture is smooth, stir the milk into it gradually with a whisk. The batter should be the consistency of thin cream; you may not have to add the entire quantity of milk. Add a pinch each of salt and sugar. Mix well with the whisk and, if some small lumps persist, strain the batter. Let it stand for 1 hour. Shortly before using it, heat the butter until it turns a very light brown *(beurre noisette),* and whisk it into the batter.

*To cook:* If possible, use two small 6-inch skillets, so that you can work faster. Heat a half teaspoon of butter in each pan, one over high heat and another over moderate heat. When the butter in the first pan is very hot, pour in enough batter just to cover the bottom of the pan (2 tablespoons or a little less—the crêpes must be very thin), and tilt the pan from side to side so the batter will cover it evenly. Cook the crêpe until the bottom is light golden brown, then turn it over and cook it for another minute. Then move the pan over to the moderate heat, and start a new crêpe in the second pan over the high heat. The crêpes should be well cooked (3 to 4 minutes each). If a crêpe should stick to the pan, slide a bit of butter under it; and butter the pans lightly as needed before starting new crêpes. As they are done, stack them one on top of the other and keep them in a warm place.

## Les Crêpes de Mon Père
*Crêpes with Whipped Cream*

Dedicated to my father

TO SERVE four:

½ recipe crêpe batter (p. 127)
¾ cup heavy cream
Granulated or confectioners' sugar to taste
1 teaspoon kirsch

MAKE THE crêpe batter and let it stand. Whip the cream until it is stiff, flavor it to taste with sugar, and add the kirsch. Chill.

At the last minute make 8 crêpes, piling them one on top of the other as they are done; be sure to keep them warm. Then spread them out, one at a time, cover half of each crêpe well with whipped cream, and fold over the other half. Serve them immediately on heated plates.

## Les Crêpes Clairette
*Flambéed Orange Crêpes*

Dedicated to our most talented and artistic daughter

TO SERVE four:

Crêpe batter (p. 127)
Grated rind of 2 oranges

>     3 tablespoons brandy
>     3 tablespoons orange liqueur, such as Cointreau *or*
>        Triple-Sec
>     3 tablespoons butter
>     3 tablespoons granulated sugar

MAKE THE crêpe batter and let it stand. Grate the thin outer rind of the orange. Combine the two liqueurs.

Cook 12 crêpes, pile them one on top of another and, when you are ready to serve the dessert, roll them into cylinders.

In a shallow flameproof serving dish or chafing dish, over moderately high heat, mix together the butter, orange rind, and sugar. Let the syrup caramelize lightly, stirring often. Then put the crêpes in the dish, pour the liqueurs over them, and touch with a lighted match. Spoon the sauce over the crêpes until the flames subside, and serve immediately.

# Les Crêpes Elisabeth
## *Flambéed Orange Crêpes with Vanilla Ice Cream*

To Elisabeth, Queen of the Belgians, beloved by her people and honored for her dedication to them, both at home and abroad

 ————————————————

TO SERVE six:

1 recipe flambéed orange crêpes (p. 129)
1½ pints VANILLA ICE CREAM (p. 163)

PREPARE 12 crêpes as in the preceding recipe for CRÊPES CLAIRETTE. However, instead of rolling the crêpes, merely fold them in halves or quarters to heat and flame them in the sauce. Then unfold a crêpe on an individual dessert plate and, with a large shallow spoon, scoop a portion of VANILLA ICE CREAM onto it. Cover with a second crêpe. Pour a spoonful of the hot sauce over this, serve immediately, and continue assembling crêpes, ice cream, and sauce until all are served.

# Les Crêpes Gallico
*Crêpes with Lemon*

TO SERVE two or three:

½ recipe crêpe batter (p. 127)
1 large lemon
2 tablespoons butter
4 tablespoons granulated sugar

MAKE THE crêpe batter and let it stand. Grate the thin outer rind of the lemon, then squeeze the juice of the lemon and strain it.

Cook 6 or 9 crêpes, pile them one on top of the other, and keep them warm.

In a shallow flameproof serving dish or a chafing dish, over moderately high heat, mix together the butter, lemon rind, and sugar. Let the syrup caramelize lightly, stirring often. Roll the crêpes into cylinders, put them in the sauce, and baste them with it until they are heated through. Serve immediately on heated plates.

# Les Crêpes Jeanlou
## *Flambéed Crêpes with Strawberries*

TO SERVE four:

½ recipe crêpe batter (p. 127)
1 pint wild strawberries, *or* small cultivated strawberries
⅜ cup granulated sugar, in all
Grated rind of 2 lemons
2 tablespoons kirsch
2 tablespoons raspberry liqueur
2 tablespoons whisky *or* brandy
Butter

MAKE THE crêpe batter and let it stand.

Rinse and hull the strawberries, drain them, and toss them
in a bowl with half the sugar. Grate the lemon rind. Combine
the three liqueurs.

Make 8 crêpes, pile them one on top of the other, and keep
them warm.

In a flameproof serving dish or in a chafing dish, over moderately high heat, mix together a generous lump of butter, the
lemon rind, and the remaining sugar. Let the syrup caramelize
lightly, stirring often.

Meanwhile, place a row of strawberries on each crêpe, and
roll them up. Arrange the crêpes in the hot lemon syrup, pour
the liqueurs over them, and touch with a lighted match. Spoon
the syrup over the crêpes until the flames subside, and serve
immediately.

# Les Crêpes Christian
*Flambéed Crêpes with Apples*

This recipe was invented for a little rascal, my godson, Christian, and later it was embellished with Calvados for the satisfaction of his older friends and relations

 ————————————

TO SERVE four:

½ recipe crêpe batter (p. 127)
2–3 fine eating apples
Granulated sugar
2 tablespoons seedless raisins
3 tablespoons butter
½ teaspoon vanilla extract
3 tablespoons Calvados *or* apple brandy

MAKE THE crêpe batter and let it stand. Peel and grate the apples, mix this pulp with sugar to taste, and stir in the raisins.

When you are ready to serve the dessert, spoon 2 tablespoons or so of the apple-raisin mixture across the center of each crêpe, and roll them up.

In a flameproof serving dish or a chafing dish, over moderately high heat, mix together the butter and 4 teaspoons of sugar. Stir well until the sugar is completely dissolved, and add the vanilla extract. Put the rolled crêpes in the hot butter and sugar and, when you are sure the dish is hot, pour the Calvados or apple brandy over them. Touch with a lighted match, spoon the sauce over the crêpes until the flames subside, and serve immediately on heated plates.

# Les Crêpes Charles
## *Flambéed Crêpes with Peaches*

Dedicated to our patron saint, the great St. Charles Bor-
romée—may he bless our efforts and continue to watch
over us

PEACH syrup is essential to this dessert. Use either
version given in the basic recipe, though the homemade syrup and cooked fresh peaches are, of course,
preferable. To stuff the crêpes, you may also use ripe
raw peaches; these should first be rolled in sugar.
To serve eight:

Crêpe batter (p. 127)
3–4 PEACHES IN SYRUP (p. 159)
3 tablespoons butter
½ cup peach syrup (p. 159)
5 tablespoons Port
5 tablespoons apricot brandy *or* orange liqueur


MAKE THE crêpe batter and let it stand. Slice the peaches if
they are cooked; raw peaches should be peeled and sliced
shortly before you are ready to serve them.

Cook 16 crêpes, pile them one on top of the other, and keep
them warm.

In a large shallow flameproof serving dish or chafing dish,
over moderately high heat, mix together the butter, peach syrup,
and Port. Let the syrup caramelize lightly, stirring often.
Meanwhile, place a few peach slices on each crêpe and roll
them up. Put the rolled crêpes in the hot syrup, and pour the
apricot brandy or orange liqueur over them. Touch with a
lighted match, spoon the sauce over the crêpes until the flames
subside, and serve immediately on heated plates.

# Les Crêpes Berthe
## *Flambéed Crêpes with Glazed Fruit*

In affectionate memory of a long friendship

TO SERVE SIX:

Crêpe batter (p. 127)
1 orange
1 lemon
1 grapefruit
1 tangerine
Confectioners' sugar
Butter
4 tablespoons granulated sugar, in all
⅜ cup Port
3 tablespoons kirsch
Grated fresh coconut

MAKE THE crêpe batter and let it stand.

Grate the outer skin of the fruit rinds; take care not to grate the white parts underneath. Then peel the fruit (the lemon may be discarded; ED), divide it into sections, and carefully remove all the white filaments and seeds. Arrange the sections in one layer in a shallow buttered pan, and sprinkle them with confectioners' or icing sugar. Cook them over high heat, turning them in a few minutes, until they acquire a brown glaze on each side.

Meanwhile, in a small saucepan combine the grated fruit rind, three quarters of the sugar, a teaspoon of butter, and the Port. Bring to a boil and cook until the mixture is slightly thickened.

Make 12 crêpes and roll them into cylinders.

In a flameproof serving dish or in a chafing dish, over moderately high heat, mix together 2 teaspoons of butter, the Port and fruit-rind mixture, and the remaining sugar. Let this sauce caramelize lightly, stirring often, then arrange the rolled crêpes in it, and surround them with the glazed fruit sections. Pour the kirsch over everything, and touch it with a lighted match. Spoon the sauce over the crêpes until the flames subside, then sprinkle with the grated coconut and serve immediately.

# Les Crêpes Marie-Claire
## *Crêpes with Candied Fruit*

Dedicated to a charming little girl, Marie-Claire Olivier, 1940–1945, who was a heroine although she never knew it

To SERVE four:

½ recipe crêpe batter (p. 127)
1 cup VANILLA PASTRY CREAM (p. 160)
¼ cup diced candied fruit
2–3 tablespoons kirsch, optional
Macaroon crumbs
Butter

MAKE THE crêpe batter and let it stand. Make the VANILLA PASTRY CREAM. Marinate the candied fruit in the kirsch; a little warm sugar syrup may be used instead of the kirsch if you wish. Crush stale or oven-dried macaroons to make fine dry crumbs.

Make 8 crêpes, pile them one on top of the other, and keep them in a warm place.

When you are ready to serve the dessert, over moderate heat melt 2 teaspoons of butter in a shallow flameproof serving dish or in a chafing dish. Spread as many crêpes as the dish will hold side by side over the butter, and heat them through. Put a spoonful of pastry cream on each one, and add a teaspoon of the candied fruit. Fold the crêpes like omelettes, sprinkle them with macaroon crumbs and, with a spatula, transfer them to individual heated dessert plates. Serve immediately, and repeat the process until everyone is served.

## Les Crêpes de l'Ambassade
### *Flambéed Stuffed Crêpes*

TO SERVE eight:

1 cup CHOCOLATE CREAM (p. 161)
1 cup VANILLA PASTRY CREAM (p. 160)
Crêpe batter (p. 127)
¼ cup finely diced pineapple, fresh or canned
Butter
Orange marmalade
¾ cup kirsch

PREPARE THE CHOCOLATE CREAM and the VANILLA PASTRY CREAM. Make the crêpe batter and let it stand. Dice the pineapple very fine.

Cook 16 crêpes, pile them one on top of the other, and keep them warm.

When you are ready to serve the dessert, butter a large flameproof baking dish and put it over low heat. Spread several crêpes in it. On one half of each crêpe put two teaspoons of the chocolate cream and then the same amount of pastry cream on the other half. Sprinkle the chocolate cream with a few bits of pineapple, roll up the crêpes, and place them at one end of the baking dish. Fill and roll the remaining crêpes in the same manner, and when they are all lined up in the dish, spread each one generously with orange marmalade.

Now turn up the heat and, when the dish is very hot, pour the kirsch over the crêpes. Touch it with a lighted match, and serve the crêpes on heated plates as soon as the flames subside.

# VIII

## Fonds de Cuisine—Viandes
*Basic Preparations—Meat*

## Fonds de Cuisine—Poissons & Crustacés
*Basic Preparations—Fish & Shellfish*

## Légumes & Garnitures
*Vegetables & Garnishes*

## Préparations Sucrées
*Basic Recipes for Desserts*

THE MANY uses for the basic recipes and *fonds de cuisine* in this chapter are explained in Chapter I, where substitutes for these preparations are also discussed.

Certain other general cooking procedures accompany recipes to which they specifically apply:

# Basic Preparations—Meat

## Clear Meat Consommé

THIS is a particularly important recipe. The consommé that is its final result is not only a delicious and digestible soup in itself (it contains no fat) but it is also the base of many other fine soups, sauces, and important dishes.

Making an absolutely perfect consommé is one of the most demanding culinary accomplishments, for it takes both time and very careful attention. We recognize that there are many who will not want to attempt it and for them we have furnished recipes for making QUICK MEAT CONSOMMÉ and CHICKEN CONSOMMÉ. Consommés can also be made with good meat extracts to be found in fine food stores, but this is a last resort, and again we cannot in all honesty say that there is anything to compare with the authentic clear meat consommé.

We give you the recipe used in our restaurant. The quantity, which will yield about 7 or 8 quarts, can be halved or quartered provided the proportions of the ingredients remain the same. Keep in mind that clear meat consommé will remain in good condition for a long time if it is kept in a cool place and that you will find it very helpful to have on hand.

4–5 leeks
3 stalks celery
5–6 large carrots
5–6 fresh tomatoes
2 large onions

6 cloves
3–4 pounds meaty beef short ribs
10–11 pounds beef bones and knuckles
Trimmings of lean beef, optional
Poultry parts (feet, wings, neck, giblets, etc.), optional
18–19 quarts water
1 sprig thyme
1 bay leaf
5 tablespoons salt
2 teaspoons peppercorns

CUT OFF the green tops of the leeks; trim the celery, removing the coarse leaves. Wash leeks, celery, carrots, and tomatoes well. Cut the leeks, celery, and carrots into large pieces. Peel the onions and stick 3 cloves into each one. Assemble the herbs and seasonings.

If poultry parts are being used, wash them well and put them in a 400° F. oven for a few minutes to extract any fat. Meanwhile, place the short ribs and bones in a large (6- to 8-gallon) kettle. Add the water, the beef trimmings, and poultry parts, and bring to a rapid boil over high heat. Using a slotted spoon, skim off any matter that comes to the surface, repeating the process at frequent intervals until no more appears. Then, and only then, add the vegetables (crushing the tomatoes as you put them in the kettle) and the herbs and seasonings. Now reduce the heat to a barely perceptible simmer and simmer thus for 5 hours, uncovered. Skim off the fat carefully and often with a spoon. Hopefully, every particle of fat will be removed.

Strain the soup into another recipient and let it cool to at least lukewarm. Meanwhile, prepare the clarifying mixture.

*To clarify consommé:*

1 pound chopped top round of beef
1 medium-size carrot

1 leek (white part only)
1 stalk celery
1 large onion
3–4 tomatoes
6 egg whites
½ teaspoon minced chervil or parsley
1 pint water

SOAK THE chopped beef, which should be free of all fat and tendons, in cold water to cover for 1 hour, and drain. Wash the carrot, leek, and celery, and peel the onion and tomatoes. Cut the vegetables into pieces, except for the onion which should be cut in half and the cut sides charred in a very hot clean skillet. Combine the meat and egg whites, put this, the vegetables, and the minced herb in a kettle large enough to contain the strained consommé as well, and add the water.

Stir the mixture together well with a whisk, then pour in the consommé. Bring to a boil over high heat, stirring constantly to prevent the egg whites from sticking to the bottom of the pan. When the soup reaches a boil, stirring is no longer necessary. Reduce the heat and simmer slowly for 1½ hours. Taste for seasoning but do not overseason.

*To strain consommé:*

RINSE A dish towel in cold water and wring it out well. Place it over an adequately large pan, tying it in place with kitchen twine unless you have an assistant to hold it in place for you. Carefully pour the consommé through the towel. You should have a clear and brilliant liquid that is a joy to behold. As a final effort, to remove the last trace of fat, pass a piece of paper tissue or toweling lightly over the surface when the consommé is lukewarm. Now bring the consommé to a final boil, pour it into containers, and let it cool completely before refrigerating.

## Quick Meat Consommé

THIS consommé can be used in place of CLEAR MEAT CONSOMMÉ but it does not have the taste, richness, or finesse. It is, however, richer and better adapted to some dishes than CHICKEN CONSOMMÉ. It is a valuable recipe in that it is made in smaller quantities and takes comparatively little time.

½ pound ground lean beef
2 egg whites
Trimmings of lean beef or veal, optional
Poultry parts (feet, wings, neck, giblets, etc.), optional
6 leeks (white parts only)
1 celery heart
1 onion
2½ tablespoons meat extract of finest quality
Pinch salt
3–4 quarts water

MIX THE ground beef with the egg whites. Place these in a 6- to 7-quart kettle. Add any extra lean beef or veal, or poultry parts, you wish. If the poultry parts are used, wash them well, and heat them in a 400° F. oven for a few minutes to extract the fat.

Wash the leeks and celery and cut them into large pieces. Peel the onions, cut them in half, and char the cut sides in a clean hot skillet. Add the vegetables, the meat extract, and the salt to the meat in the kettle, and cover with cold water. Stirring constantly, bring the mixture to the boiling point. Then reduce the heat and simmer, uncovered, for 1½ hours. Strain this consommé as in the preceding recipe.

## *Chicken Consommé*

One 4- or 5-pound chicken or hen
1 onion
2 cloves
1 stalk celery
2 leeks (white parts only)
2 carrots
1 small sprig thyme
½ bay leaf
1 tablespoon salt
½ teaspoon white peppercorns
3–4 quarts water

PUT THE chicken or hen, which has been drawn (and singed, if necessary), into a kettle; add the giblets, well cleaned. Add the onion, peeled and spiked with the cloves, the rest of the vegetables, well washed and cut in pieces, and the herbs and seasonings. Cover with cold water, bring to a boil, and simmer slowly, half covered, for 6 hours. Carefully skim off the fat as it appears on the surface.

Strain and cool, and remove any fat that remains. Refrigerate only after the consommé has cooled thoroughly.

## *Meat Jelly*

MEAT JELLY, or *glace de viande,* is one of the most important elements of cookery. It is the basis of many fine sauces and is usually the specialty of a highly trained chef. But there is no reason why the amateur cannot make it provided he is willing to devote the time and care that is required. The result will be a jelly that adds to many dishes a rich and perfect flavor unequalled by any commercial substitute. Besides, this jelly keeps in perfect condition for quite a long time. Concentrated meat extracts sold in fine-foods stores can, of course, be used. But it stands to reason that one cannot expect to obtain with these products the flavor of the authentic recipe. It must also be remembered that commercial extracts are highly seasoned and that consequently they must be used sparingly in any dish to which they are added. (This difficulty is particularly evident in the commercial meat "extracts" and "glazes" that are most readily available in our stores. However, some specialty shops do carry *glace de viande* of high quality —salted, to be sure, but it is by all means the best product to use if you do not make your own. ED.)

Below is the recipe used in our restaurant. Note that *no* salt is added to it. Anyone making this for home use may want to halve the ingredients; the full recipe yields close to a quart of meat jelly. To store it, pour it while it is still warm into sterilized earthenware crocks or heavy glass jars, and let it cool completely before putting it in the refrigerator.

The making of the jelly has two phases: (1) making the stock and (2) reducing it to a jelly.

10–11 pounds veal knuckles
10–11 pounds beef bones, including knuckles
3 pounds lean beef (preferably on a knuckle bone)
2 large onions
4 cloves
2 pounds large carrots
3 stalks celery
6 leeks
¼ pound butter

1 pint tomato purée,* *or* 3 pounds fresh tomatoes
Bouquet garni (1 sprig thyme, 1 bay leaf, 3 sprigs
    parsley)
16–17 quarts cold water
Boiling water as needed

*First phase:*

ASK THE butcher to saw and pound the bones. More fresh meat
(beef or veal, but never pork, mutton, or lamb) besides the beef
already prescribed may be added to great advantage. Especially
good are chicken or a hen, and beef or calves' feet, liver, and
lights (all these must be washed thoroughly).

Place the broken bones in a large shallow pan and cook
them over a high flame or in a hot oven so that they will
brown all over; stir them from time to time to prevent charring.
This process contributes a fine flavor and seals in some of the
albumen, lessening the amount of scum that will later form
on the bouillon during the boiling.

Peel and halve the onions, sticking each half with a clove.
Char the cut sides in a clean hot skillet. Wash the carrots,
celery, and leeks, discarding most of the green parts of the leeks.
Cut the vegetables into 2-inch pieces, and sauté them in the
butter until they are gilded all over.

Put the browned bones, the fresh meat, and the vegetables,
including the tomato purée or fresh tomatoes, in a 5- to 6-gallon
kettle. Add the cold water, making sure that all the ingredients
are covered. Add the *bouquet garni,* tied with twine. Simmer
all together for 4 hours, skimming the surface of the stock from
time to time to remove the grey matter that will float to the top.

Here, allow us to make a suggestion. The lean meat is now
removed and it may be served for a family meal in either of
two ways: Served hot, it should be accompanied by freshly
boiled potatoes or other vegetables and hot mustard; served

* See p. 6 concerning tomato purée.

cold, it should be sliced thin, arranged on a platter, surrounded with sliced cold boiled potatoes, sprinkled with chopped parsley, and sauced with a fine mayonnaise. A green salad or one of fresh tomatoes go very well with this.

With the lean pieces of meat removed, the bouillon should continue to simmer for 10 hours. The ten hours need not be continuous; four hours one day and six the next may be more convenient. But it is important that the bouillon be allowed to cool *completely* before it is stored in the refrigerator in the interim. During the hours of simmering, two important steps must be taken: (1) There must be a careful and regular skimming of the surface of the stock, removing as much fat as possible; (2) *the level of the liquid must be maintained at all times* by adding boiling water periodically.

### Second phase:

POUR THE liquid through a fine strainer into a smaller kettle, thus removing all bones and solid particles. Now boil down the bouillon over a moderately high flame, but, as it reduces, lower the heat gradually. And, as the volume of the liquid is reduced, it is also advisable to transfer it to progressively smaller saucepans. It is to be reduced to approximately 1 quart.

The test for discovering when the jelly is *à point* is to dip a spoon into the liquid: If it adheres to the spoon, the jelly has reached the proper density. A fork test is made by dipping the tines into the liquid: A pearl of jelly should form at the end of each tine, and these should coagulate immediately when they are dropped on a cold plate. When it is lukewarm, the jelly should resemble a thick syrup; when it is cold, it will become a very stiff jelly.

# Basic Preparations—Fish & Shellfish

## *Court-Bouillon for Fish*

ONE OF the preferred methods of cooking fish is to poach it in a *court-bouillon* which can be prepared in advance and used when it is needed. This recipe is for a small fish; since fish must always be completely covered by liquid when it is cooked in this manner, larger ones will require a *court-bouillon* proportionately larger in volume. The *court-bouillon* must be cool or lukewarm when the fish is put into it, then brought to a simmer and simmered gently until the fish is done.

The same ingredients are used for boiling lobster, but for this they do not have to be cooked in advance (see page 62).

1 small onion
1 shallot
1 carrot
1 stalk celery
2 tablespoons butter
2 cups dry white wine
4 cups water
1 sprig thyme
1 bay leaf
3 sprigs parsley
Juice of 1 lemon
2 cloves
1 tablespoon salt
1 teaspoon peppercorns

PEEL THE onion and shallot, wash the carrot and celery, and slice them all thinly. Put them in a 2-quart saucepan with the butter, and place over moderate heat. Cook slowly until the vegetables are very soft but not browned. Add the wine, water, and lemon juice, and all the herbs and seasonings except the peppercorns. Bring to a boil, boil for 15 minutes, remove from the stove, and let cool for 15 minutes. Then add the peppercorns and let stand 10 minutes longer. Then pour the *court-bouillon* through a fine strainer and, if it is not to be used immediately, store it in earthenware crocks or in glass jars in a cool place.

## Concentrated Fish Stock

CONCENTRATED fish stock, or *fumet de poisson,* is used in many fish recipes to give added flavor. Once prepared, it can be stored in the refrigerator to be used in the small quantities usually required. Housewives may want to halve or quarter the recipe. The trimmings (heads, tails, bones, etc.) of any white fish are acceptable but those of flat fish such as flounder, sole, dab, turbot, or brill are preferable.

10 pounds fresh fish trimmings
5–6 sprigs parsley
2 sprigs thyme
2 bay leaves
1 celery heart
1 onion, *stuck with*
2 cloves
1½ tablespoons salt
½ bottle good dry white wine
8½ quarts water

PUT ALL the ingredients in a large kettle, bring to a rolling
boil, and boil hard for 15 minutes; skim thoroughly. Then reduce the heat and simmer gently for 3 hours. Pour the stock
through a fine strainer, then boil it down until it thickens
slightly. The liquid, over all, will have reduced to a little less
than half the original quantity.

## *Lobster Bisque Base*

THIS basic preparation is one of our most important
inventions and makes the difference in many of our
dishes between good and superb cooking. And it is
used, of course, to make our LOBSTER BISQUE. The
full recipe below, which can easily be halved, yields
6 pints or more.

Two 1½-pound live lobsters
2 medium carrots
1 celery heart
1 medium onion
1 shallot
2 pounds fresh tomatoes
2 tablespoons chopped parsley
1 bay leaf
Pinch of thyme
6 tablespoons olive oil, in all
4 tablespoons butter
3 quarts plus 1 cup CONCENTRATED FISH STOCK
  (p. 150)
2 cups tomato purée *

* See p. 6 concerning tomato purée.

1 teaspoon salt

2 teaspoons ground pepper

2 cups heavy cream

FIRST PREPARE a *mirepoix:* Wash and scrape the carrots and celery; peel the onion and shallot. Plunge the tomatoes into boiling water, remove and peel them, cut them in two, and press out the seeds. Dice all the vegetables quite fine, and combine them. Put three fourths of this mixture in a large heavy pan with the herbs, 4 spoonfuls of the oil, and the butter. Cook over a moderate flame, stirring occasionally, for 20 minutes or until the vegetables are soft.

Meanwhile, separate the claws from the lobsters and divide the bodies from the tails with a heavy sharp knife or small cleaver. Split each piece in two and carefully remove the tomalley (liver) from the bodies. Keep this in reserve.

Add all the lobster pieces to the *mirepoix* and continue cooking until the shells turn bright red, stirring frequently with a large wooden spoon. When all the pieces are red, add the CONCENTRATED FISH STOCK (or, lacking that add consommé or, less acceptably, water), and add the tomato purée, pepper, salt, and the tomalley. Mix well and simmer all gently together for 20 minutes. Remove the lobster pieces with a slotted spoon.

Preheat the oven to 450° F. Remove the lobster meat from the shells, cutting the shells as necessary, and put the meat aside. Put the shells on a baking sheet and heat them in the oven until they are dry; this will heighten the flavor they impart to the final bisque. Do not let them scorch. Pound the shells as fine as possible in a mortar (or break them up and pulverize them in an electric blender). Place them in a small saucepan with the remaining 2 spoonfuls of oil and the rest of the diced vegetables.

Cook this mixture gently for 20 minutes, then add it to the liquid in which the lobsters cooked. Now add the cream, mix well, add the lobster meat, and cook all together again gently for about 20 minutes, or until the sauce is thick, stirring frequently. Pass the mixture through a fine strainer several times, discarding the lobster meat and the shells. Taste for seasoning and pour the bisque base into earthenware crocks or glass jars. It will become very thick when cool. Store, covered, in the refrigerator only after it is completely cool.

# Vegetables & Garnishes

## *How to Prepare Whole Mushrooms*

 ——————————

CARE must be taken that no sand or dirt is left in the mushrooms. Choose mushrooms that are very fresh and as white as possible. Using a sharp knife, trim them and remove all particles of dirt. Just before cooking, wash the mushrooms carefully, drain them, pat them dry with a towel, and cut off the stems. Once the mushrooms are washed, it is important to cook them immediately.

If mushrooms are used often, it is wise to prepare and cook a good supply to have on hand.

1 pound mushrooms
¼ cup water
3 tablespoons butter
1 teaspoon salt

PUT ALL the ingredients in a saucepan and boil for 5 to 7 minutes. Transfer the mushrooms and their juice to a glass or ceramic bowl, and let cool before storing in the refrigerator.

## Mushroom Duxelles

THIS preparation is often called for in fine dishes and lends a very special flavor. Since it is called for in varying amounts, I give you the recipe for ½ pound of mushrooms which will yield about half a cupful of *duxelles*. This can easily be doubled if necessary.

Clean, wash, and mince the mushrooms. Place them in a piece of cheesecloth or clean toweling and twist them into a ball, squeezing very hard to remove all the water.

In a small saucepan, heat together 2 teaspoons each of butter, minced shallot, and minced onion. Cook over moderate heat for about 3 minutes, or until the vegetables are tender but not browned. Add the mushrooms, and cook over low heat until the mixture is almost dry. Season lightly with salt and pepper.

## How to Prepare Artichokes

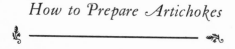

CHOOSE the freshest artichokes possible. Trim them at the stem ends and cut off the top thirds with a very sharp knife or scissors. Wash the artichokes thoroughly and tie each with a piece of kitchen string. Plunge them into a kettle of boiling salted water, boil until the outer leaves tear off easily, then drain them well.

Force the leaves apart, without breaking them off, in order to twist out the chokes in the centers. If only the artichoke bottoms are to be used, remove the leaves as well as the chokes.

Artichoke bottoms are available in tins and may usually be used as substitutes for fresh ones. They should be carefully rinsed and dried. For hot dishes, tinned or fresh, they should be heated in a little butter over a low flame before they are used.

## *How to Cook Truffles*

COOKING fresh truffles is not, I understand, a problem that comes up often in American or English kitchens, but for those who have an interest in such things, I am including this recipe. If you are using tinned truffles, restore their flavor by marinating them in a little Madeira added to the truffle juice in the tin.

Good truffles must be absolutely fresh, not too woody in texture, and as free from cracks as possible. Ideally, they are perfectly round. The best truffles are of French origin (the Périgord, the Vaucluse) and others of a different variety also come from Italy (Umbria, Piedmont).

Truffles can be cut to create many kinds of garnish. If they are cut into tiny pieces, they require no cooking in advance and are added to a dish during its last minutes of cooking. Otherwise they are cooked in the following manner.

1 pound fresh truffles
3 tablespoons mixed minced vegetables (carrot, onion, celery)
1 tablespoon butter
Madeira *or* Port

REMOVE EVERY bit of dirt from the truffles, soaking them first in lightly salted lukewarm water (1 teaspoon of salt to 1 quart of water) for 45 minutes. Then drain them and scrub them with a stiff-bristled brush until they are perfectly clean; keep cold water running over them as you scrub.

In a heavy pan, simmer the mixed minced vegetables in the butter until they are soft. Add the truffles and enough wine to come a quarter of the way up the truffles. Cook them, covered, over low heat for about 20 minutes; do not overcook them. Then slice or dice them, or cut them into rounds or strips, as suits the dish they are to accompany. Reserve the cooking liquid.

## *Duchesse Potatoes*

DUCHESSE potatoes are used as a garnish for meat, chicken, or fish. The prepared potato pureé is put in a pastry bag while it is still hot and piped around the edge of the platter through tips of various sizes and shapes. If the potato mixture is not to be used immediately, use *only the yolks* of the eggs in the recipe and not the whites.

To garnish a platter that is to serve four:

1 pound potatoes
3 tablespoons butter
2 eggs
Salt and pepper
Nutmeg, optional

PEEL AND quarter the potatoes, and boil them in salted water until tender; they must be entirely covered with water. Drain the potatoes well and force them through a strainer or ricer. Dry the purée by putting it back over moderate heat for a few minutes, stirring with a wooden spoon. Add the butter, salt and pepper, and nutmeg. Remove from the fire and add the eggs, mixing carefully and thoroughly.

If the mixture is not to be used immediately, put it in a buttered bowl, cover it with a buttered paper, poke a small hole in the paper, and let cool. (As a rule, this cooled purée is then later shaped by hand to make the desired garnish. ED.)

## *Boiled Rice or Rice Ring*

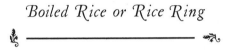

To SERVE three or four: Bring 2 quarts of water to a full rolling boil. Add 2 teaspoons of salt. Pour ½ pound of well-washed rice into the boiling water; boil about 18 minutes. Drain the rice in a colander and immediately wash it under cold running water, stirring gently. Drain completely.

Reheat, in a fireproof casserole with a lump of butter, for 15 to 20 minutes in a 350° F. oven. Or pack the rice firmly in a well-buttered ring mold and reheat in the same manner; turn the rice out onto a heated platter.

# Basic Recipes for Desserts

## How to Prepare Cherries in Syrup

THIS preparation is basic to our cooking and is used in several dishes other than desserts. Anyone who plans to use our recipes would do well to make this preparation in larger quantities when cherries are in season and to preserve some of it. In some recipes, only the cherry syrup is called for.

2 pounds sound sour cherries
3 cups granulated sugar
¾ cup water
2 tablespoons Port
2 tablespoons sherry
2 tablespoons brandy

WASH THE cherries carefully and remove the stems. Dissolve the sugar in the water over moderate heat, stirring. Increase the heat and bring to a boil. Throw in the cherries and boil them 3 to 5 minutes, depending on their size. Then strain the cherry syrup into another pan, and cook it down rapidly until it thickens. Remove from the heat, add the cherries, and add the wines and brandy. Cool at room temperature and store in a cool place.

To preserve this preparation, place in glass jars, cap, seal, and sterilize for 25 minutes in boiling water.

*To substitute tinned sour cherries:* The syrup may have to be augmented and fortified. Add a fairly dense prepared sugar syrup to the cherries, heat but do not boil, add the wines and brandy, and cool.

## *How to Prepare Peaches in Syrup*

THESE peaches and their syrup serve as ingredients in other dishes, therefore this is considered a basic recipe. However, peaches prepared in this way make an excellent dessert, peeled and served cold or warm, with some of the syrup. They may also be served with a CHOCOLATE CREAM, VANILLA PASTRY CREAM, or VANILLA ICE CREAM.

6–8 peaches, preferably white
1 quart water
3 cups granulated sugar
Vanilla bean
2 tablespoons brandy *or* kirsch

COMBINE THE cold water and sugar in a casserole that will also hold the peaches. Stir together until the sugar is dissolved, and add a piece of vanilla bean. Place over high heat, bring to a boil, and add the peaches, well washed but not peeled. Cook until the peaches are soft. Remove a peach with a slotted spoon to test it; if it is slightly soft to the touch, it is done. Remove all the peaches when they are done, remove the vanilla bean, and leave the syrup to boil down until it is quite thick. Add the brandy, kirsch, or whisky. Cool and store in well corked bottles.

*If you must substitute tinned peaches:* Try to find white peaches, though, admittedly, they are not often available and yellow peaches may have to do. In any case, the syrup will have to be improved.

Boil together until reduced and thickened, the strained peach syrup and half its quantity of sugar. Then measure it and flavor it in approximately the following proportions:

¾ cup reduced peach syrup
¼ cup Port, Madeira, or sherry
2 teaspoons apricot liqueur, kirsch, or brandy

Cool and store in a corked bottle as you would the fresh peach syrup.

## *How to Prepare Vanilla Pastry Cream*

VANILLA pastry cream may be kept, tightly covered, in the refrigerator for several days and used in a variety of different desserts. However, if the proportions given below make more than you can use, they can easily be halved. ED.

1 quart milk
Vanilla bean, *or* 1 tablespoon vanilla extract
4 teaspoons flour
6 egg yolks
⅞ cup granulated sugar
Pinch of salt
1½ tablespoons sweet butter

BOIL THE milk, with a vanilla bean, if possible; otherwise, add the vanilla extract later.

In a large bowl, combine the flour and a few spoonfuls of additional cold milk, and mix well to form a smooth not-too-thick paste. With a whisk, beat into this the egg yolks, one by one, and the sugar and salt. When the mixture is well blended, beat in a cupful of the boiling milk, then pour the egg mixture slowly back into the hot milk, stirring constantly. (Remove the vanilla bean, or, if you did not use one, now add the vanilla extract.) Stir the pastry cream over moderate heat until it is smooth and thickened but do not let it come to a boil. Remove from the heat, add the butter, and stir until it melts.

## *How to Prepare Chocolate Cream*

5 teaspoons Dutch cocoa
¼ cup granulated sugar
3 cups heavy cream

IN A heavy saucepan, mix together thoroughly the cocoa and sugar. Add a teaspoon of water, and mix to a paste. Place over moderate heat, gradually add the cream, and stir with a whisk until the mixture is well blended. Then increase the heat, and keep stirring until the cream thickens. It tends to boil over easily, so the pan will have to be lifted from the heat from time to time. When the mixture bubbles thickly and you see that the cream is considerably reduced, remove it from the heat and pour it into a china or earthenware bowl. Cool completely before storing in the refrigerator.

If the chocolate cream is to be used immediately, put the bowl in a larger bowl of cracked ice, and stir until the cream is cold.

The amount of cream in this recipe may be varied—less cream for a more strongly chocolate flavored sauce, more cream for a milder one; the cooking time will vary accordingly. The recipe, of course, may easily be halved.

## *How to Prepare Sugar Syrup for Sherbet*

WE use in making sugar syrup an instrument, called a *pèse-syrop* or saccharometer, which measures the density of the syrup. To make sherbets or water ices, the syrup meter should read 15° (note that this is a measure of density and not of temperature). As you may not have this instrument, you will have to judge for yourself whether the syrup is too thick and needs to have a little boiling water added to it or whether, on the contrary, it needs a little more sugar (which should be dissolved in a little boiling water before it is added to the syrup). However, if you use the proportions of sugar and water indicated, there should be no trouble.

1¾ cups granulated sugar
4¼ cups cold water


IN A saucepan, combine the sugar and cold water, and stir until the sugar is completely dissolved. Then put over heat and bring to a boil. Remove from the heat and let the syrup cool completely. It may then be tested with the syrup meter, which should read 15°.

## *How to Make Vanilla Ice Cream*

VERY GOOD ice cream is, of course, commercially available. No matter how fine it is, however, a good homemade ice cream is invariably better. We give our recipe here without instructions for freezing it, as these will depend on the equipment you have. (An ice-cream freezer, whether hand-driven or electrically powered, gives better results than freezing in a refrigerator freezer. ED.) The quantities given are for somewhat less than 2 quarts of ice cream.

1¼ cups granulated sugar
8 egg yolks
Pinch of salt
4¼ cups milk
Vanilla bean, *or* 1 tablespoon vanilla extract
2 tablespoons sweet butter
2 cups heavy cream

IN A heavy enameled saucepan, combine the sugar, egg yolks, and salt. Beat well with a whisk until the mixture is smooth and thickened and falls in ribbonlike strands from the whisk.

Put the milk and the vanilla bean, if you have one, in another saucepan and bring to a boil. Remove the vanilla bean, and pour the hot milk gradually into the sugar-and-egg mixture, beating constantly with a whisk. Place over moderate heat and cook, still beating constantly, until the mixture thickens into a light custard; do not let it boil. Then stir in the butter, which will stop the cooking, and the vanilla extract if you did not use a vanilla bean, and remove immediately from the heat. Let the custard cool, then add the cream and beat together well.

# Index